Lighthouses
of
Nova Scotia
by Harold Stiver

Copyright Statement

Lighthouses of Nova Scotia
A Guide for Photographers and Explorers

Published by Harold Stiver
Copyright 2025 Harold Stiver

Table of Contents

Tours

A Short History of Lighthouses

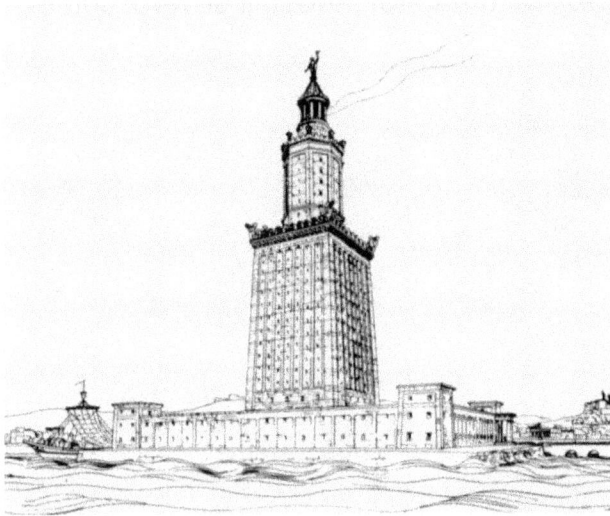

There is some evidence of a lighthouse from the 5th century B.C. of Themistocles of Athens constructing a stone column with a fire on top. This was at the harbour of Piraeus, associated with Athens.

However one of most famous and spectacular early structures was the Lighthouse of Alexandria, or the Pharos of Alexandria. It was one of the Seven Wonders of the Ancient World.

The lighthouse was built in the Third Century B.C. in Alexandria, Egypt by Ptolemy II. It stood on the island of Pharos in the harbour of Alexandria and was said to be 110 metres (350 feet) high.

The lighthouse was built in three stages, a large square at the bottom, an octagonal layer in the middle, and a cylindrical tower at the top.

The structure lasted until a series of earthquakes damaged it, with the 1303 Crete earthquake resulting in its destruction.

The Tower of Hercules, in northwest Spain, is modelled after the Pharos Lighthouse.

The first lighthouse in Canada was built in 1734 in Louisbourg on Cape Breton Island, Nova Scotia. Over the years, the structure was damaged beyond repair in a battle between the British and the French in 1758, destroyed by fire in 1923 and had to be rebuilt several times. The lighthouse known today was built in 1923.

Currently Canada's oldest surviving lighthouse is Sambro Island Lighthouse, built in 1758 at the entrance to Halifax Harbour. It is seen in the image above. It is also the oldest in North America.

Nova Scotia County Map

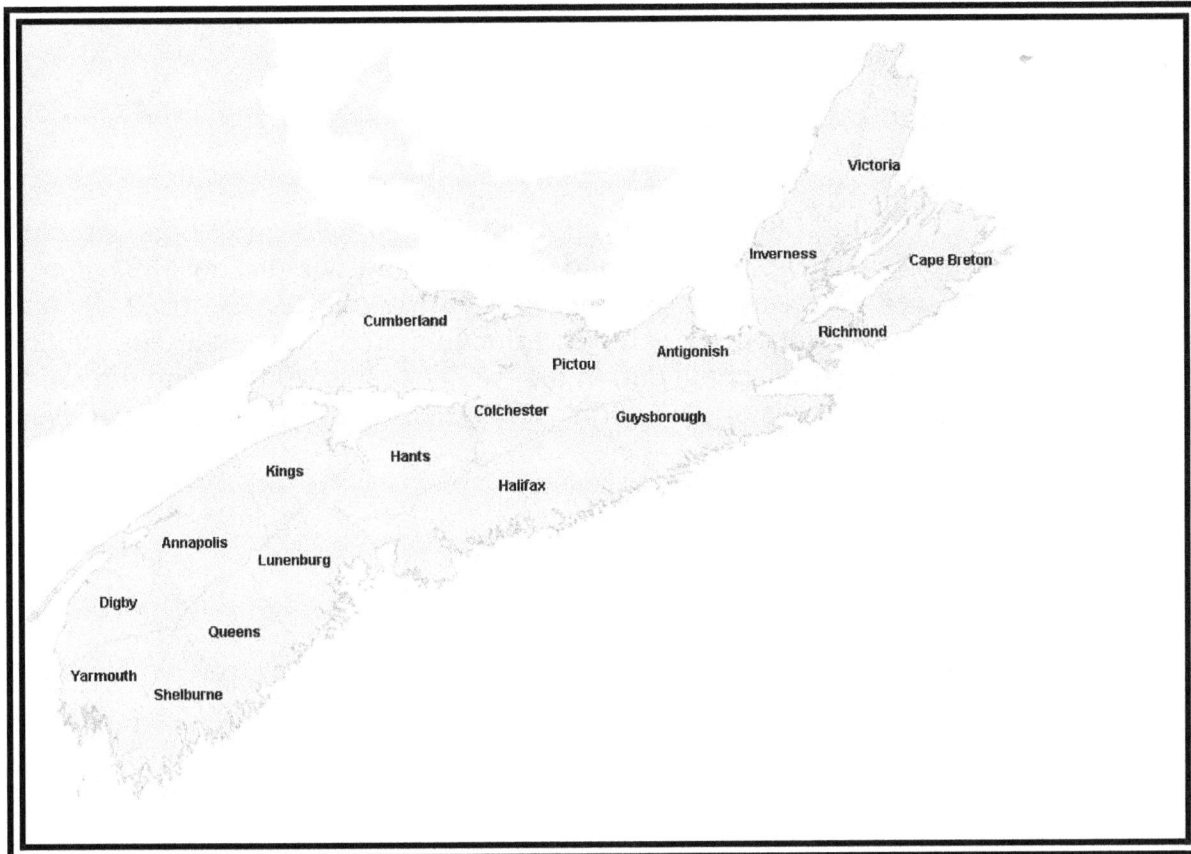

Abbotts Harbour Lighthouse

In 1884, a light on a mast was opened on Abbots Island to aid vessels entering Abbott's Harbour and in 1891 it was relocated near the Harbour entrance. In 1922 it was replaced by a tower relocated from Amherst. The station was discontinued in the 1990s and in 2004 it was moved to the Historical Acadian Village of Nova Scotia in Lower West Pubnico.

Description: Square pyramidal wood tower

Location: Pubnico

Directions: 91 Old Church Rd, Lower West Pubnico

Coordinates: 43°38'21.3"N 65°47'34.8"W

Opened: 1922

Automated: 1966

Deactivated: 2004

Height: 9 meters, 30 feet

Focal Height: 11 meters, 37 feet

Signal: Fixed green

Foghorn signal: N/A

Visitor Access: Grounds open, tower closed (Admission)

Annapolis Lighthouse

The Annapolis Lighthouse was erected in 1889 for ships entering the Annapolis River. The site is owned by The Historical Association of Annapolis Royal and is headquarters for tours. The lighthouse was restored in 2016.

Description: White, square pyramidal wooden tower

Location: Annapolis Royal

Directions: 247 St George St, Annapolis Royal

Coordinates: 44°44'39.6"N 65°31'11.8"W

Opened: 1889

Automated: Not known

Deactivated: Active

Height: 8.5 meters, 28 feet

Focal Height: 9 meters, 30 feet

Signal: Fixed red

Foghorn signal: N/A

Visitor Access: Grounds open, tower closed

Apple River Lighthouse

The original Apple River Lighthouse was erected in 1848 to aid ships at the entrance to the Apple River. The light was lost to fire in 1869 but by 1870 it was replaced by a tower erected by John Livingstone. In 1899 a fog alarm was added to the site. The current tower opened in 1972 and continues to be active.

Description: White square tower

Location: Apple River

Directions: From Apple River, head NW on Apple River Road for 4.5 km where you can view the site across the bay.

Coordinates: 45°28'25.5"N 64°51'16.9"W

Opened: Original 1870, Current 1972

Automated: 1972

Deactivated: Active

Height: 10.5 meters, 35 feet

Focal Height: 21.5 meters, 71 feet

Signal: White flash every 12 seconds

Foghorn Signal: Blast every 60 seconds

Visitor Access: Grounds open, tower closed

Arisaig Lighthouse

The Arisaig Lighthouse is a replica of an 1898 lighthouse which burned in 1939. Local volunteers erected this replica in 2007 with support from government. Parking and information displays are provided for visitors.

Description: Square pyramidal wood tower

Location: Arisaig

Directions: From Airsaig, head NW on NS-245 E for 800 meters and turn left onto Arisaig Point Rd where the site is 750 meters

Coordinates: 45°45'42.8"N 62°10'19.9"W

Opened: 2007

Automated: N/A

Deactivated: N/A

Height: 8 meters, 26 feet

Focal Height: N/A

Signal: N/A

Foghorn signal: N/A

Visitor Access: Grounds open, tower open in season

Baccaro Point Lighthouse

The original Baccaro Point Lighthouse was erected in 1851 to aid vessels travelling near Barrington Bay. Black circles were painted on three sides as a distinguishing daymark. It was destroyed in a 1934 fire. The current tower was erected that same year as a replacement. The station was restored in 2016 by local volunteers with grants funding it.

Description: White, square pyramidal tower

Location: Baccaro

Directions: From Baccaro, head SW on Baccaro Rd toward for 900 meters and turn left onto Lighthouse Rd where you will find the site in 800 meters

Coordinates: 43°26'59.0"N 65°28'15.0"W

Opened: Original 1851, Current 1934

Automated: 1984

Deactivated: Active

Height: 13.5 meters, 44 feet

Focal Height: 16 meters, 52 feet

Signal: 3 white flashes every 10 seconds

Foghorn: Discontinued in 2014 (Was blast every 20 seconds)

Visitor Access: Grounds open, tower closed

Balache Point Range Lights

Cape Breton Island is separated from the mainland of Nova Scotia by the Canso Strait and it is in heavy use by thousands of ships each year. The original Balache Point Light was built in 1905 to protect vessels in the narrow portion of the strait nearby. It was discontinued when the causeway was finished. In 1963 a set of range lights was built on Balache Point at the northern entrance. The front range was replaced by a skeleton tower in 1991.

Front Range

Description: Square skeleton tower

Location: Port Hastings

Rear Range: (Image above)

Description: Square pyramidal wood tower

Location: Port Hastings

Directions: From Port Hastings, head west on Trans-Canada Hwy/NS-104 W for 450 meters and turn right for the site on an unnamed road.

Coordinates: 45°38'57.7"N 61°24'59.4"W

Opened: Original 1905, Current 1991

Automated: 1991

Deactivated: Active

Height: 3.5 meters, 11 feet

Focal Height: 6 meters, 20 feet

Signal: Red flash every 11 seconds

Visitor Access: Closed

Coordinates: 45°38'52.9"N 61°24'51.8"W

Opened: Original 1905, Current 1963

Automated: 1963

Deactivated: Active

Height: 6 meters, 20 feet

Focal Height: 9 meters, 30 feet

Signal: Red flash every 11 seconds

Visitor Access: Closed

Bass River Lighthouse

The Bass River Lighthouse was built in 1907 at the west side of the entrance to Bass River and was initially a free standing tower, It was deactivated in 1992 and sold into private hands two years later. The new owner built a house around the tower.

Description: Square pyramidal wood tower attached to residence

Location: Bass River

Directions: Take Wharf Road south from NF-2 for 1.6 km to find the site

Coordinates: 45°23'42.7"N 63°46'53.2"W

Opened: 1907

Automated: 1973

Deactivated: 1992

Height: 10 meters, 30 feet

Focal Height: 12.5 meters, 41 feet

Signal: Fixed white

Foghorn Signal: N/A

Visitor Access: Closed (Viewable from shoreline)

Battery Point Breakwater Lighthouse

The original Battery Point Lighthouse was opened in 1864. In 1937 the Battery Point Breakwater Lighthouse was erected at the end of the breakwater that was off Battery Point. In 1951 a new breakwater was built and the current tower was placed at the tip of it. While you cannot go onto the breakwater, it is easy to view the site from shore.

Description: Square pyramidal wood tower

Location: Lunenburg

Directions: Head south on Battery Point Rd from Blue Rocks Road east of Luneneburg for 550 meters where the lighthouse can be viewed.

Coordinates: 44°21'36.8"N 64°17'47.3"W

Opened: Original 1864, Second 1937, Current 1951

Automated: 1993

Deactivated: Active

Height: 7 meters, 24 feet

Focal Height: 25 meters, 81 feet

Signal: Fixed red

Foghorn signal: Fog horn (Discontinued in 1992)

Visitor Access: Grounds open, tower closed

Bear River Lighthouse

The Bear River Lighthouse was opened in 1905 on Winchester Point at the entrance to Bear River. It was automated in 1973 and deactivated in 2001. The contractor was John Roney. Bear River Lighthouse was listed as a heritage lighthouse in 2015.

Description: Square pyramidal wood tower

Location: Digby

Directions: From Smith's Cove, head NE on Hwy 1/Nova Scotia Trunk 1 E for 1.8 km to find the site.

Coordinates: 44°37'01.0"N 65°41'06.7"W

Opened: 1905

Automated: 1973

Deactivated: 2001

Height: 9 meters, 30 feet

Focal Height: 19.5 meters, 64 feet

Signal: Fixed red

Foghorn signal: N/A

Visitor Access: Grounds open, tower closed

Belliveau Cove Lighthouse

The original Belliveau Cove Lighthouse was built in 1889 as an aid to ships travelling to Belliveau Cove. By 1973 the tower was in poor shape and was blown over in a storm. The local community built a replica of the original in the 1980s and have operated it privately since then.

Description: Square pyramidal wood tower

Location: Belliveaus Cove

Directions: From Belliveaus Cove, head north on Nova Scotia Trunk 1 E for 130 meters and view the site off the coast

Coordinates: 44°23'20.4"N 66°03'49.6"W

Opened: Original 1889, Current 1980s

Automated: 1980s

Deactivated: Active

Height: 6.5 meters, 21 feet

Focal Height: 6 meters, 20 feet

Signal: White flash every 8 seconds

Foghorn Signal: N/A

Visitor Access: Grounds open, tower closed

Berry Head (Tor Bay) Lighthouse

The original Berry Head Lighthouse was built by James McDonald in 1876 to note Berry Head and the western entrance to Tor Bay. The site was replaced with a new tower and dwelling in 1951. The light was automated in 1959 and the unused buildings were destroyed in 1972. The current tower was erected in 1985 and remains active.

Description: Square tower ascending from the fog signal building

Location: Tor Bay

Directions: From Tor Bay, head east on Tor Bay Branch Rd for 2.3 km and turn right to stay on Tor Bay Branch Rd were the site is 3.0 km

Coordinates: 45°11'28.8"N 61°18'39.9"W

Opened: Original 1876, Second 1959, Current 1985

Automated: 1985

Deactivated: Active

Height: 5.5 meters, 19 feet

Focal Height: 12.5 meters, 41 feet

Signal: Fixed white

Foghorn Signal: 3 blasts every 60 seconds

Visitor Access: Grounds open, tower closed

Betty Island Lighthouse

n 1873 the RMS Atlantic hit an underwater rock west of Betty Island. 535 people perished in the worst loss of life wreck in the North Atlantic to that point. In 1875 the original Betty Island Lighthouse was built by Mr. Baker under a Department of Marine contract. In 1939 the second tower replaced the light with a two story dwelling with a lantern room on top. In 1981, Blunden Construction Ltd built the current tower and the second tower was destroyed in 1986.

Description: Square pyramidal wood tower

Location: Terence Bay

Directions: Accessible by boat

Coordinates: 44°26'19.7"N 63°46'00.4"W

Opened: Original 1875, Second 1939, Current 1981

Automated: 1985

Deactivated: Active

Height: 9 meters, 30 feet

Focal Height: 19 meters, 63 feet

Signal: White flash every 15 seconds

Foghorn Signal: Blast every 60 seconds

Visitor Access: Grounds open, tower closed

Black Rock Lighthouse

The original Black Rock Lighthouse was opened in 1848 as an aid to ships using the Midas Channel near Grafton. The current fiberglass tower replaced it in 1967. It continues to be active.

Description: White cylindrical tower

Location: Harbourville

Directions: From Black Rock, head west on Black Rock Rd for 300 meters and find the site.

Coordinates: 45°10'13.2"N 64°45'42.6"W

Opened: Original 1848, Current 1967

Automated: 1993

Deactivated: Active

Height: 10 meters, 34 feet

Focal Height: 16 meters, 52 feet

Signal: 2 white flashes every 10 seconds

Foghorn Signal: N/A

Visitor Access: Grounds open, tower closed

Black Rock Point Lighthouse

The original Black Rock Point Lighthouse was built by Robert Purves in 1868. The light aids ships travelling the northern entrance to the Great Bras d'Or Channel from St. Ann's Bay. The current lighthouse replaced the original in 1978. Parks Canada recognized Black Rock Point Lighthouse as a heritage lighthouse in 2017.

Description: White, square tower attached to fog building

Location: Big Bras d'Or

Directions: From Black Rock, head NW on Black Rock Light Rd for 600 meters to find the site

Coordinates: 46°18'18.8"N 60°23'31.4"W

Opened: Original 1868, Second 1937, Current 1978

Automated: 1990

Deactivated: Active

Height: 10.5 meters, 35 feet

Focal Height: 23.5 meters, 77 feet

Signal: Continuous sector light, white, red or green depending on direction

Foghorn signal: Blast every 30 seconds

Visitor Access: Grounds open, tower closed

Boars Head Lighthouse

The original Boars Head Lighthouse was erected in 1864 on Long Island to mark the entrance to Petit Passage which is the shortest route between St. John and Yarmouth. In 1910 a fog alarm was added to the site. The tower was replaced by the current one in 1957. The site was automated in 1987 and is still active.

Description: Square pyramidal wood tower

Location: Tiverton

Directions: From the west terminal of the Tiverton-East Ferry, head NW on Boars Head Rd for 1.1 km and find the site

Coordinates: 44°24'14.5"N 66°12'55.0"W

Opened: Original 1864, Current 1957

Automated: 1987

Deactivated: Active

Height: 10.5 meters, 35 feet

Focal Height: 18 meters, 60 feet

Signal: White flash every 5 seconds

Foghorn Signal: 3 blasts every 60 seconds

Visitor Access: Grounds open, tower closed

Bordens Wharf Lighthouse

The Bordens Wharf Lighthouse opened in 1904 to aid ships travelling the Habitant River leading to Canning. The site was built under contract by Mr. Wm. Rand. The lighthouse has an interesting history. It was deactivated in 1921. In 1959 the bottom portion was taken to house pigs on a farm and in 1980 it was moved to act as a storage shed. In 1990 it was relocated to a riverbank in Canning where it was restored and used as an information centre.

Description: Square pyramidal wood tower

Location: Canning

Directions: Habitant River in Canning

Coordinates: 45°09'26.5"N 64°25'20.2"W

Opened: 1904

Automated: N/A

Deactivated: 1921

Height: 6 meters, 20 feet

Focal Height: 9 meters, 29 feet

Signal: Fixed red

Foghorn Signal: N/A

Visitor Access: Grounds open, tower closed

Brier Island Lighthouse

The original Brier Island Lighthouse was opened in 1809 to protect ships from hazards at the entrance of St. Mary's Bay. It was rebuilt in 1832 due to decay in the original and a fog signal was added at that time. It was destroyed in a fire in 1944 when the present tower was built. It was automated in 1987 and continues to be active.

Description: White octagonal tower

Location: Westport

Directions: From Westport, head SW on Lighthouse Rd for 3.6 km to find the site.

Coordinates: 44°14'55.0"N 66°23'32.0"W

Opened: Original 1809, Second 1832, Current 1944

Automated: 1987

Deactivated: Active

Height: 18 meters, 60 feet

Focal Height: 29 meters, 95 feet

Signal: 3 white flashes every 24 seconds

Foghorn signal: 2 blasts every 60 seconds

Visitor Access: Grounds open, tower closed

Bunker Island Lighthouse

The original Bunker Island Lighthouse was built by Francis Ryerson and opened in 1874 as an aid to ships travelling to Yarmouth Harbour. A replacement tower was built in 1924. A keeper's dwelling was added in 1885 as previously he lived on shore and stay all night at the lantern room. The current tower was added in1960 and remains active.

Description: Square cylindrical concrete tower

Location: Yarmouth

Directions: East side of Yarmouth Harbour

Coordinates: 43°48'44.3"N 66°08'35.6"W

Opened: Original 1874, Second 1924, Current 1960

Automated: 1981

Deactivated: Active

Height: 9 meters, 30 feet

Focal Height: 10 meters, 32 feet

Signal: Fixed red

Foghorn: Added in 1885

Visitor Access: Grounds open, tower closed

Burntcoat Head Lighthouse

The original Burntcoat Head Lighthouse was built by Mr. Carter and opened in 1859. It was built to aid ships travelling the Minas Basin. Due to erosion, this tower was replaced by one situated 152 meters to the east in 1913. This was replaced by a light on a pole in 1972 and this was also deactivated a few years later. Local citizens wished to have a lighthouse return and in 1995 a replica of the of the 1913 light was opened as part of a plan for ecotourism.

Description: Original Octagonal lantern on the roof of square keeper's house, Second skeleton tower, Current Replica of original

Location: Burntcoat

Directions: 611 Burntcoat Rd, Noel

Coordinates: 45°18'40.9"N 63°48'21.5"W

Opened: Original 1859, Second 1914, Current 1995

Automated: 1975

Deactivated: 1970s

Height: 12 meters, 39 feet

Focal Height: 23 meters, 76 feet

Signal: Fixed white

Foghorn signal: N/A

Visitor Access: Grounds open, tower open mid May to mid October

Canso Range Lights

In 1905 the Canso Range Lights were opened to aid mariners travelling to Canso Harbour. E. F. Munro was the contractor. The concrete foundations were renewed for both towers in 2008 and the front tower was moved back from the coast. Both towers continue to be active.

Front Range

Description: Square pyramidal wood tower

Location: Canso

Directions: From Canso, head east on Union St for 650 meters and turn right onto Wilmot St to find the site

Coordinates: 45°19'56.2"N 60°58'46.5"W

Opened: 1905

Automated: 1958

Deactivated: Active

Height: 8.5 meters, 28 feet

Focal Height: 10 meters, 34 feet

Signal: Fixed yellow

Visitor Access: Closed

Rear Range (Image above)

Description: Square pyramidal wood tower

Location: Canso

Coordinates: 45°19'55.7"N 60°59'01.4"W

Opened: 1905

Automated: 1958

Deactivated: Active

Height: 17 meters, 56 feet

Focal Height: 28.5 meters, 94 feet

Signal: Fixed yellow

Visitor Access: Grounds open, tower closed

Cape d'Or Lighthouse

The Cape d'Or station opened in 1874 and in 1922 a lighthouse in Eatonville was relocated to become the original Cape d'Or Lighthouse. The current lighthouse was built in 1965 and was made up of a fog signal building with a light tower erected from one corner. The light continues to be active.

Description: White square tower

Location: Advocate Harbour

Directions: From East Advocate, head south on Back St for 1.1 km and turn right onto Cape Dor Rd where the site is 5.6 km

Coordinates: 45°17'23.7"N 64°46'28.9"W

Opened: Original 1922, Current 1965

Automated: 1989

Deactivated: Active

Height: 7 meters, 22 feet

Focal Height: 24 meters, 80 feet

Signal: White flash every 6 seconds

Foghorn signal: 2 blasts every 60 seconds

Visitor Access: Grounds open, tower closed

Cape Forchu Lighthouse

The original Cape Forchu Lighthouse opened in 1840 as an aid to ships travelling to Yarmouth Harbour. In 1908 the lighting was upgraded with a 2nd order Fresnel lens. In 1962 the current lighthouse replaced the original. The lighthouse was automated in 1993, the last Nova Scotia station to be destaffed. It continues to be active.

Description: Hexagonal tower

Location: Yarmouth

Directions: From Cape Forchu, head south on NS-304 for 1.9 km and the site

Coordinates: 43°47'38.8"N 66°09'19.3"W

Opened: Original 1840, Current 1962

Automated: 1993

Deactivated: Active

Height: 23.5 meters, 77 feet

Focal Height: 35 meters, 114 feet

Signal: White flash every 12 seconds

Foghorn Signal: Blast every 60 seconds

Visitor Access: Grounds open, tower close

Cape George Harbour Lighthouse

The original Cape George Harbour Lighthouse was opened in 1875 as an aid to ships travelling from Bras d'Or Lake to to Cabot Strait. Duncan McRae performed the building of the site. The current tower was erected as a replacement in 1950 by H.E. McDonald. The lighthouse was listed as a Heritage Lighthouse in 2020.

Description: Square pyramidal wood tower

Location: French Cove

Directions: From Cape George, head east on Oldys Rd for 1.8 km to find the site

Coordinates: 45°44'05.2"N 60°48'38.1"W

Opened: Original 1875, Current 1950

Automated: 1960

Deactivated: 2013

Height: 8 meters, 27 feet

Focal Height: 12.5 meters, 41 feet

Signal: White flash every 4 seconds

Foghorn signal: N/A

Visitor Access: Grounds open, tower closed

Cape George Lighthouse

The original Cape George Lighthouse was built in 1861 for ships entering St. Georges Bay from the northwest. In 1908 a wooden, octagonal lighthouse was erected to replace the original tower as well as a new keeper's dwelling with the work completed by E.F. Munro. A 3rd order Fresnel lens upgraded the lighting. The current tower was built by Northumberland Construction Ltd and opened in 1968. It is still active.

Description: Octagonal concrete tower

Location: Ballantynes Cove

Directions: From Ballantynes Cove, head northeast on Lighthouse Rd from Sunrise Trail and in 700 meters, find the site

Coordinates: 45°52'26.8"N 61°54'01.8"W

Opened: Original 1861, Second 1908, Current 1968

Automated: 1993

Deactivated: Active

Height: 14 meters, 45 feet

Focal Height: 123 meters, 404 feet

Signal: 3 white flashes every 12 seconds

Foghorn signal: N/A

Visitor Access: Grounds open, tower closed

Cape Roseway Lighthouse

The original Cape Roseway Lighthouse was opened in 1788, the second lighthouse built in Nova Scotia. A new dwelling was built in 1833, replacing very poor accommodation previously. A fog alarm building was added to the site in 1883. The tower was damaged in a fire in 1959 and the current tower opened as a replacement in 1961, built by Cameron Contracting Ltd.

Description: Octagonal concrete tower

Location: Shelburne

Directions: Accessible by boat

Coordinates: 43°37'21.4"N 65°15'50.0"W

Opened: Original 1788, Current 1961

Automated: 1986

Deactivated: Active

Height: 14.5 meters, 48 feet

Focal Height: 33 meters, 108 feet

Signal: White flash every 10 seconds

Foghorn: Discontinued 1989

Visitor Access: Grounds open, tower closed

Cape Sable Lighthouse

Request for a lighthouse on Sable Island were made as early as 1841 but the wreck of the SS Hungarian on the cape with the loss of all 205 people prompted the plans to go forward. The original Cape Sable Lighthouse opened in 1861, as an aid to ships travelling to the western entrance to Barrington Bay. A fog alarm was added to the site in 1876. In 1902 a 3rd order Fresnel lens upgraded the lighting. The current tower is the tallest in Nova Scotia at 101 feet.

Description: White, octagonal reinforced concrete tower

Location: Clark's Harbour

Directions: Accessible by boat

Coordinates: 43°23'24.7"N 65°37'15.7"W

Opened: Original 1861, Current 1924

Automated: 1986

Deactivated: Active

Height: 31 meters, 101 feet

Focal Height: 30 meters, 98 feet

Signal: White flash every 5 seconds

Foghorn Signal: Blast every 60 seconds

Visitor Access: Grounds open, tower closed

Cape Sharp Lighthouse

The original Cape Sharp Lighthouse was opened in 1886 to guide ships through Minas Basin. A 6th order lens produced a fixed red light. A foghorn was added to the site in 1899. The current lighthouse opened in 1973, The station was automated in 1988 and continues to be active.

Description: Square pyramidal wood tower

Location: Parrsboro

Directions: The lighthouse is at the end of Pleasure Cove Lane, a rough single lane road

Coordinates: 45°21'51.9"N 64°23'32.4"W

Opened: original 1886, Current 1973

Automated: 1988

Deactivated: Active

Height: 10.5 meters, 35 feet

Focal Height: 18 meters, 60 feet

Signal: White flash every 10 seconds

Foghorn Signal: Blast every 60 seconds

Visitor Access: Grounds open, tower closed

Cape St. Marys Lighthouse

The original Cape St. Marys Lighthouse opened in 1868 as a guide into St. Mary's Bay. A fog control building was added to the station in 1915. The current lighthouse was opened in 1969. It was automated in 1988 and continues to be active.

Description: Square cylindrical concrete tower

Location: Mavillette

Directions: From Mavillette, head SW on Cape St Marys Rd for 2.6 km and turn right onto Lighthouse Rd where the site is a short distance.

Coordinates: 44°05'09.5"N 66°12'39.7"W

Opened: Original 1868, Current 1969

Automated: 1988

Deactivated: Active

Height: 8.5 meters, 28 feet

Focal Height: 31.5 meters, 104 feet

Signal: White flash every 5 seconds

Foghorn Signal: Blast every 60 seconds

Visitor Access: Grounds open, tower closed

Caribou Lighthouse

The original Caribou Lighthouse was built by Robert Purves and opened in 1868. In 1877 it was moved inland due to erosion. The second Caribou Lighthouse was built by W. Talbot and opened in 1915. The current tower was built in 1971 as well as a fog control building. It was automated in 1990 and continues to be active.

Description: White square tower

Location: Caribou

Directions: From Caribou River, head east on R Grant Rd for 2.7 km aand turn right onto Shore Rd. After 1.0 km, make a sharp left onto Caribou Island Rd and the site is 9.6 km

Coordinates: 45°45'53.2"N 62°40'50.3"W

Opened: Original 1868, Second 1916, Current 1971

Automated: 1990

Deactivated: Active

Height: 12.5 meters, 40 feet

Focal Height: 13 meters, 44 feet

Signal: 3 white flashes every 20 seconds

Foghorn: Fog signal established, 1968

Visitor Access: Grounds open, tower closed

Carter Island Lighthouse

The original Carter Island Lighthouse was built in 1872 by James A. Hayden as an aid to ships entering Lockeport Harbour. A new dwelling and tower were opened in 1930, as well as a fog control building and boathouse. The current lighthouse opened in 1982. It was automated and continues to be active.

Description: Round fiberglass tower

Location: Lockeport

Directions: Accessible by boat

Coordinates: 43°42'19.3"N 65°06'04.0"W

Opened: Original 1872, Second 1930, Current 1982

Automated: 1982

Deactivated: Active

Height: 9 meters, 31 feet

Focal Height: 16.5 meters, 54 feet

Signal: White flash every 6 seconds

Foghorn: Fog signal established 1918

Visitor Access: Grounds open, tower closed

Caveau Point Range Lights

The quick red fox jumped over the lazy brown dog. The quick red fox jumped over the lazy brown dog. The quick red fox jumped over the lazy brown dog. The quick red fox jumped over the lazy brown dog. The quick red fox jumped over the lazy brown dog. The quick red fox jumped over the lazy brown dog. The quick red fox jumped over the lazy brown dog. The quick red fox jumped over the lazy brown dog. The quick red fox jumped

Front Range

Description: Skeleton tower

Location: Cheticamp

Directions: From Cheticamp, head north on NS-30 toward for 550 meters to find the site

Coordinates: 46°38'56.6"N 61°00'6.00"W

Opened: 1976

Automated: 1993

Deactivated: Active

Height: 6.5 meters, 21 feet

Focal Height: 17 meters, 56 feet

Signal: Fixed red

Visitor Access: Closed

Rear Range (Image above)

Description: Square pyramidal wood tower

Location: Cheticamp

Coordinates: 46°38'54.7"N 60°59'51.5"W

Opened: 1990

Automated: 1993

Deactivated: Active

Height: 8 meters, 27 feet

Focal Height: 17 meters, 56 feet

Signal: Fixed red

Visitor Access: Closed

Charlos Harbour Rear Range Light

The original Charlos Harbour Range Lights were erected by the Department of Marine in 1901 as an aid to vessels travelling to Charlo Harbour. The lights were deactivated in 1988. The front tower has been demolished. Local volunteers have restored the Rear Range Light.

Description: Square pyramidal wood tower

Location: Charlos Cove

Directions: From Larrys River, head north on Marine Dr/NS-316 S for 4.8 km to find the site

Coordinates: 45°14'48.3"N 61°19'39.8"W

Opened: Original 1901, Current 1965

Automated: Not known

Deactivated: 1988

Height: 7.5 meters, 25 feet

Focal Height: 15.5 meters, 51 feet

Signal: Fixed white

Foghorn signal: N/A

Visitor Access: Closed

Chebucto Head Lighthouse

The original Chebucto Head Lighthouse was opened in 1872 to help ships to safely enter Halifax Harbour. The contract was completed by Jacob Bowser. The Sambro Lighthouse's fog-whistle was moved to the Chebucto Head Lighthouse around 1890. In 1930 a new lighthouse was erected as a replacement but it was demolished during WW2 for a gun battery. In 1940 a new dwelling with a lantern room on top was built. The current lighthouse was completed in 1967.

Description: White, octagonal concrete tower

Location: Halifax

Directions: From Duncans Cove, head east on Chebucto Head Rd/Duncans Cove for 2.2 km to find the site

Coordinates: 44°30'26.6"N 63°31'21.4"W

Opened: Original 1872, Second 1928, Current 1940

Automated: 1980

Deactivated: 1967

Height: 14 meters, 45 feet

Focal Height: 49 meters meters, 162 feet

Signal: White flash every 20 seconds

Foghorn Signal: 2 blasts every 60 seconds

Visitor Access: Grounds open, tower closed

Cheticamp Harbour Front Range Light

Range lights were established at Cheticamp Harbour in 1890 in the form of lanterns on masts. In 1894 towers were erected to replace the masts. When the dredged channel was moved in 1914, the towers were relocated. When the lights were deactivated in 1986. the front range tower became part of the marina, and is now painted in the form of an Acadian flag.

Description: Square pyramidal wood tower

Location: Cheticamp

Directions: 15311 Cabot Trail, Cheticamp

Coordinates: 46°37'56.8"N 61°00'40.1"W

Opened: 1894

Automated: 1980

Deactivated: 1986

Height: 7 meters, 23 feet

Focal Height: 14 meters, 45 feet

Signal: Fixed red

Foghorn signal: N/A

Visitor Access: Grounds open, tower open

Coffin Island Lighthouse

The original Coffin Island Lighthouse was opened in 1815, the fifth lighthouse in Nova Scotia. It was destroyed in a 1913 fire and replaced with the second tower in 1914. This tower suffered from erosion and eventually the foundation was undermined. The current tower opened in 2006. It remains active.

Description: Fiberglass tower

Location: Liverpool

Directions: Accessible by boat

Coordinates: 44°02'01.1"N 64°37'41.8"W

Opened: Original 1815, Second 1914, Current 2006

Automated: 1962

Deactivated: Active

Height: 16 meters, 52 feet

Focal Height: 18.5 meters, 61 feet

Signal: White flash every 4 seconds

Foghorn: Established 1871

Visitor Access: Grounds open, tower closed

Coldspring Head Lighthouse

The Coldspring Head Lighthouse opened in 1890 as an aid to ships travelling by Baie Verte along Northumberland Strait. The tower was built by J. Harvey Brownell who also became the first keeper. It was deactivated in 2013. In 2015, Cold Spring Head Lighthouse was listed as a Heritage Lighthouse.

Description: Square pyramidal wood tower

Location: Amherst Shore

Directions: From Amherst Shore, head NW on Cold Spring Head Rd off NS-366 for 550 meters and turn right onto Rivers Wood Loop, then left onto Lobster Cove Ln to find the site

Coordinates: 45°57'44.7"N 63°51'54.6"W

Opened: 1890

Automated: 1980

Deactivated: 2013

Height: 11 meters, 36 feet

Focal Height: 18 meters, 60 feet

Signal: White flash every 5 seconds

Foghorn signal: N/A

Visitor Access: Grounds open, tower closed

Cranberry Islands Lighthouse

In 1807 the House of Assembly of Nova Scotia proposed that a lighthouse be built at Cranberry Island to mark the entrance to Canso Harbour. The original Cranberry Islands Lighthouse opened in 1818. In 1865 fog trumpets were added to the site. In 1929 the tower was replaced by a square concrete tower. In turn this tower was replaced in 1978 by a white square tower attached to fog signal building. It was automated in 1986.

Description: Octagonal tower

Location: Canso

Directions: Accessible by boat

Coordinates: 45°19'29.6"N 60°55'38.2"W

Opened: Original 1929, Current 1978

Automated: 1986

Deactivated: Active

Height: 14.5 meters, 48 feet

Focal Height: 17 meters, 55 feet

Signal: White flash every 15 seconds

Foghorn Signal: Blast every 60 seconds

Visitor Access: Grounds open, tower closed

Cross Island Lighthouse

Cross Island divides the entrance to Lunenburg Harbour info two channels with the south being safer. A lighthouse was proposed for Cross Island and it opened in 1832. A foghorn was added to the site in 1879. In 1960 the tower and fog alarm building were destroyed in a fire. It was replaced by an aluminum tower and in 1980 the current tower replaced that. The light was automated in 1989 and remains active.

Description: Circular fibreglass tower

Location: Lunenburg

Directions: Accessible by boat

Coordinates: 44°18'43.7"N 64°10'06.4"W

Opened: Original 1832, Second 1960, Current 1980

Automated: 1989

Deactivated: Active

Height: 11.5 meters, 38 feet

Focal Height: 25 meters, 82 feet

Signal: White flash every 10 seconds

Foghorn signal: 2 blasts every 60 seconds

Visitor Access: Grounds open, tower closed

Devils Island Lighthouse

Devils Island is the furthermost island in Halifax Harbour. In 1877, the Devils Island Lighthouse was built by Jacob Bowser to mark the approach to Halifax Harbour. The light was automated in 1967 and the remaining buildings were sold. The light was removed from the tower early in 2009.

Description: Octagonal wood tower

Location: Halifax

Directions: Accessible by boat

Coordinates: 44°34'51.7"N 63°27'28.1"W

Opened: 1877

Automated: 1967

Deactivated: 1978

Height: 12 meters, 39 feet

Focal Height: 16 meters meters, 52 feet

Signal: White flash every 10 seconds

Foghorn Signal: N/A

Visitor Access: Grounds open, tower closed

Digby Pier Lighthouse

The original light shown from the Digby Pier was a lantern on a mast showing a fixed red signal. In 1903 the Digby Pier Lighthouse replaced it with the contract fulfilled by John Roney. It initially had a 7th order lens but the lighting was upgraded to a 5th order lens in 1915. The light was deactivated and moved to the city of Saint John to be part of the Market Slip area. In 2012 the lighthouse was returned to Digby and placed in storage. In 2015 funds became available to restore it and it was moved to its current location on the waterfront.

Description: Square pyramidal wood tower

Location: Digby

Directions: Just east of Church and Water streets in Digby

Coordinates: 44°37'20.5"N 65°45'20.1"W

Opened: Original 1887, Current 1902

Automated: Not known

Deactivated: 1971

Height: 8 meters, 26 feet

Focal Height: 9 meters meters, 30 feet

Signal: White flash every 15 seconds

Foghorn signal: N/A

Visitor Access: Grounds open, tower closed

East Ironbound Island Lighthouse

The original East Ironbound Island Lighthouse was opened in 1867 to guide ships travelling the eastern entrance to Mahone Bay. The station was destroyed by fire likely caused by lightning in 1870. Hopps and Brown built the current lighthouse which opened in 1871 and is the fifth-oldest surviving lighthouse in Nova Scotia. A 4th order Fresnel lens upgraded the lighting in 1912. East Ironbound Lighthouse was listed as a Recognized Federal Heritage Building in 2006

Description: Square cylindrical wood tower

Location: Mahone Bay

Directions: Accessible by boat

Coordinates: 44°26'22.4"N 64°04'59.7"W

Opened: Original 1867, Current 1871

Automated: 1990

Deactivated: Active

Height: 11 meters, 35 feet

Focal Height: 44.5 meters, 146 feet

Signal: White flash every 6 seconds

Foghorn: Foghorn discontinued 1929

Visitor Access: Grounds open, tower closed

Enragee Point Lighthouse

The original Enragee Point Lighthouse opened in 1937. This lighthouse was destroyed in a fire in 1956. A replacement opened in 1957. It has been listed as a Heritage Lighthouse in 2010.

Description: White, octagonal concrete tower

Location: Cheticamp

Directions: From NS-30 south of Cheticamp, head west on Cheticamp Island Rd for 1.7 km and turn right onto Du Phare/Gallant Rd. You find the site in 6.1 km

Coordinates: 46°38'58.4"N 61°01'35.2"W

Opened: Original 1937, Current 1957

Automated: 1988

Deactivated: Active

Height: 13 meters, 32 feet

Focal Height: 22.5 meters, 74 feet

Signal: 3 white flashes every 24 seconds

Foghorn signal: Blast every 30 seconds

Visitor Access: Grounds open, tower closed

Five Islands Lighthouse

The Five Islands Lighthouse was built by A. L. Mury in 1913. Due to erosion, the tower was moved 3 times, in 1952, 1957 and 1996. In 2008 it was moved again, to a parcel of land where a park was built by the county.

Description: Square pyramidal wood tower

Location: Five Islands

Directions: Head south on Broderick Ln from NS-2 east of Moose River for 800 meters and the site.

Coordinates: 45°24'15.9"N 64°05'17.3"W

Opened: 1914

Automated: 1967

Deactivated: 1993

Height: 10 meters, 33 feet

Focal Height: 13 meters, 43 feet

Signal: Flashing red

Foghorn Signal: N/A

Visitor Access: Grounds open, tower open July and August

Flint Island Lighthouse

The original Flint Island Lighthouse opened in 1856 as a coastal light as well as an aid to vessels travelling to Cow Bay and Bridgeport. The lighthouse was destroyed in an 1864 fire and a replacement opened in 1866. A fog alarm building was added to the station in 1908. The following year saw the 3rd lighthouse built on the site. The current tower was opened in 1962 and continues to be active.

Description: White hexagonal tower

Location: Donkin

Directions: Accessible by boat

Coordinates: 46°10'51.0"N 59°46'13.2"W

Opened: Original 1856, Current 1962

Automated: 1982

Deactivated: Active

Height: 18 meters, 59 feet

Focal Height: 21 meters, 70 feet

Signal: 2 white flashes every 20 seconds

Foghorn signal: Blast every 30 seconds

Visitor Access: Grounds open, tower closed

Fort Point Lighthouse

The Fort Point Lighthouse was opened in 1855 to aid vessels travelling to Liverpool Harbour. It is the third oldest lighthouse surviving in Nova Scotia. A hand foghorn was added to the station in 1901. The light was deactivated in 1989 and Queen's County Museum plans to use the lighthouse as a gift shop.

Description: Square pyramidal wood tower

Location: Liverpool

Directions: Off the end of Fort Point Road in Liverpool

Coordinates: 44°02'36.6"N 64°42'27.3"W

Opened: 1855

Automated: 1989

Deactivated: 1989

Height: 5 meters, 17 feet

Focal Height: 9 meters, 30 feet

Signal: Fixed white

Foghorn Signal: Hand-cranked fog horn

Visitor Access: Grounds open, tower open from June 1 to September 1

French Point (Musquodoboit Harbour Rear Range) Lighthouse

In 1904 the French Point Lighthouse opened as part of a set of range lights. It is also known as the Musquodoboit Harbour Rear Range. The lights are intended to guide vessels travelling to anchor at Steering Beach. The range lights were automated in 1951. The front range tower was removed in 2010.

Description: Square pyramidal wood tower

Location: Pleasant Point

Directions: Head northwest on Kent Rd from Ostrea Lake Road north of Pleasant Point for 400 meters and walk NW towards the coast for 400 meters and the site.

Coordinates: 44°42'21.1"N 63°04'33.4"W

Opened: 1904

Automated: 1951

Deactivated: 1980

Height: 9.5 meters, 31 feet

Focal Height: 14 meters, 47 feet

Signal: Fixed red

Foghorn signal: N/A

Visitor Access: Grounds open, tower closed

Gabarus Lighthouse

The Gabarus Lighthouse opened in 1891 to aid ships entering Gabarus Harbour. It was built by Neil McNiell. In 2015 the tower was moved inland away from the eroding cliff. Gabarus Lighthouse was listed as a Recognized Federal Heritage Building in 2007.

Description: Square pyramidal wood tower

Location: Gabarus

Directions: Take Harbour Point Road off NS-327 for 650 and you find the site

Coordinates: 45°50'36.5"N 60°08'50.5"W

Opened: 1891

Automated: 1964

Deactivated: Active

Height: 9.5 meters, 31 feet

Focal Height: 16.5 meters, 54 feet

Signal: Fixed red

Foghorn signal: N/A

Visitor Access: Grounds open, tower close

Georges Island Lighthouse

In 1857 local Halifax business owners requested a harbour lighthouse for Georges Island but it was not until 1876 before the original Georges Island Lighthouse was opened. It was built by Mr. Thomas Halliwell. A fog bell was added to the station in 1899. In 1916 the tower was destroyed by fire and a temporary light was signaled from the dwelling. In 1919 the current lighthouse was opened, equipped with a 4th order Fresnel lens. Georges Island was listed as a National Historic Site in 1965.

Description: Octagonal concrete tower

Location: Halifax

Directions: Accessible by boat, Distant view from Halifax waterfront

Coordinates: 44°38'25.8"N 63°33'37.4"W

Opened: Original 1876, Current 1917

Automated: 1972

Deactivated: Active

Height: 16.5 meters, 54 feet

Focal Height: 17.5 meters, 58 feet

Signal: Fixed white

Foghorn Signal: Blast every 30 seconds

Visitor Access: Closed

Gilberts Cove (Gilbert Point) Lighthouse

The Gilberts Cove Lighthouse was opened in 1904 to serve ships travelling St. Mary's Bay. The building was erected by Mr. John Roney. The light was automated in 1965 and discontinued in 1975. In 1982 a group was formed to restore the site. They have a museum, gift shop, and tea room in the lighthouse now.

Description: Square cylindrical wood tower rising from the roof of the keeper's dwelling

Location: Gilberts Cove

Directions: From Gilberts Cove, head southwest on NS-101 W for 500 meters and turn right onto Lighthouse Rd and the site is 1.2 km

Coordinates: 44°29'39.2"N 65°57'08.8"W

Opened: 1904

Automated: 1965

Deactivated: 1975

Height: 11.5 meters, 38 feet

Focal Height: 12 meters, 40 feet

Signal: Fixed red

Foghorn Signal: N/A

Visitor Access: Grounds open, tower open mid-June to late-September

Gillis Point Lighthouse

The Department of Marine for Nova Scotia decided to put a lighthouse at Gillis Point as an aid to ships entering Maskells Harbour and the Gillis Point Lighthouse opened in 1895. Cummings Construction Ltd renovated the tower in 1978 and the dwelling was removed. The light was deactivated in 2011. The station was listed as a Heritage Lighthouse in 2017.

Description: Square pyramidal wood tower

Location: Iona

Directions: From Gillis Point, head NW on Gillis Point Rd for 3.3 km to find the site.

Coordinates: 46°01'23.6"N 60°46'39.3"W

Opened: 1895

Automated: 1967

Deactivated: 2011

Height: 11 meters, 37 feet

Focal Height: 22.5 meters, 74 feet

Signal: White flash every 4 seconds

Foghorn Signal: N/A

Visitor Access: Grounds open, tower close

Grand Passage Lighthouse

The original Grand Passage Lighthouse was opened in 1901 to aid mariners travelling through the northwest Grand Passage entrance. This tower served for many years but was replaced by the current tower in 1965. The lighthouse was listed as a Heritage Lighthouse in 2021.

Description: Square cylindrical concrete tower

Location: Westport

Directions: From Westport, head north on Water St for 2.2 km to find the site

Coordinates: 44°17'13.0"N 66°20'31.2"W

Opened: Original 1901, Current 1965

Automated: 1988

Deactivated: Active

Height: 8.5 meters, 28 feet

Focal Height: 14.5 meters, 47 feet

Signal: White flash every 10 seconds

Foghorn: Fog bell added 1903

Visitor Access: Grounds open, tower closed

Grandique Point Lighthouse

The original light at Grandique Point was a pole light which helped ships travelling the east entrance to the Lennox Passage. This was updated to the current Grandique Point Lighthouse in 1907. The tower was moved inland in 1963 and 2010 due to erosion. The light continues to be active.

Description: Square pyramidal wood tower

Location: Martinique

Directions: From Lennox, head east on Fleur-de-lis Trail/NS-320 E for 200 meters and turn left onto Grandique Rd where the site is 900 meters

Coordinates: 45°35'38.2"N 61°01'19.8"W

Opened: Original 1884, Current 1907

Automated: 1961

Deactivated: Active

Height: 8.5 meters, 25 feet

Focal Height: 9 meters, 29 feet

Signal: Fixed green

Foghorn Signal: N/A

Visitor Access: Grounds open, tower closed

Great Bras d'Or Range Lights

Range Lights were needed to help mariners find the correct path to the entrance of the Great Bras d'Or Channel leading to Bras d'Or Lake. In 1903 this set of lights were opened after the construction was done by P. L. McFarlane. Their signal was changed frpm fixed white to fixed green in 1956 and automated in 1958. Both towers remain active.

Front Range (Image above)

Description: Square pyramidal wood tower

Location: Big Bras d'Or

Directions: From Big Bras d'Or, head north on Old Rte 5 2.8 km and turn left onto Browns Ln where the site is 300 meters

Coordinates: 46°17'25.5"N 60°24'48.3"W

Opened: 1903

Automated: 1958

Deactivated: Active

Height: 9.5 meters, 32 feet

Focal Height: 16 meters, 52 feet

Signal: Fixed green

Foghorn Signal: N/A

Visitor Access: Closed

Rear Range

Description: Square pyramidal wood tower

Location: Big Bras d'Or

Coordinates: 46°17'12.3"N 60°24'59.1"W

Opened: 1903

Automated: 1958

Deactivated: Active

Height: 16 meters, 54 feet

Focal Height: 19 meters, 63 feet

Signal: Fixed green

Foghorn Signal: N/A

Visitor Access: Closed

Green Island (Chebogue Point) Lighthouse

The station on Green island off Yarmouth opened as a fog alarm site in 1919. It was not until 1964 that the light was added as protection against a lengthy rock ledge south of Green Island. The light continues to be active.

Description: Square tower, white, on square concrete building

Location: Rockville

Directions: Accessible by boat

Coordinates: 43°41'23.1"N 66°08'38.3"W

Opened: 1964

Automated: 1981

Deactivated: Active

Height: 6 meters, 20 feet

Focal Height: 25 meters, 82 feet

Signal: White flash every 5 seconds

Foghorn Signal: Blast every 20 seconds

Visitor Access: Closed

Guyon Island Lighthouse

The original Guyon Island Lighthouse was built by John G. Sinclair and opened in 1877 as an aid to ships travelling to the entrance of Forchu Bay. A fog alarm building was added to the site in 1923 with a bridge to the keeper's dwelling. The current tower replaced the original in 1964 along with new keeper's dwellings. The light was automated in 1984 and continues to be active.

Description: Hexagonal pyramidal wood tower

Location: Gabarus

Directions: Accessible by boat

Coordinates: 45°45'57.3"N 60°06'45.7"W

Opened: Original 1877, Current 1964

Automated: 1984

Deactivated: Active

Height: 13 meters, 45 feet

Focal Height: 216 meters, 53 feet

Signal: White flash every 20 seconds

Foghorn Signal: Blast every 60 seconds

Visitor Access: Grounds open, tower closed

Hampton Lighthouse

The Hampton Lighthouse was built in 1911 by J. F. Titus and is privately owned and operated. The lighting is a 6th order Fresnel lens. Hampton Lighthouse was listed as a Provincial Heritage Property in 2007.

Description: Square pyramidal wood tower

Location: Hampton

Directions: From Hampton, head NE on Shore Rd E for 350 meters and turn left onto Hampton Wharf Rd and the site is 300 meters

Coordinates: 44°54'21.8"N 65°21'00.8"W

Opened: 1911

Automated: 1957

Deactivated: Active

Height: 10 meters, 33 feet

Focal Height: 21 meters, 69 feet

Signal: Fixed white

Foghorn Signal: N/A

Visitor Access: Grounds open, tower open Saturdays and Sundays from July through mid-September

Hart Island Lighthouse

In 1872 the original Hart Island Lighthouse was opened to aid ships entering Canso Harbour. It was situated on the eastern portion of hart's or Cutler's Island. In 1909 a 5th order lens was added to upgrade the lighting. In 1929 the current tower, composed of a dwelling and lighthouse replaced the original. When the current tower was deactivated in the 1960s, its lantern room was removed.

Description: Circular tower

Location: Canso

Directions: Accessible by boat

Coordinates: 45°20'37.6"N 60°59'25.3"W

Opened: Original 1872, Current 1929

Automated: 1936

Deactivated: 1960s

Height: 10 meters, 33 feet

Focal Height: 13 meters, 42 feet

Signal: Fixed red

Foghorn signal: N/A

Visitor Access: Closed

Havre Boucher Range Lights

The Department of Marine budgeted for range lights to mark the entrance to Havre Boucher Harbour and Wm. Kaulback was given the contract. The current rear range tower was erected in 2010 and used a vinyl cover that looked like wood but would not require as much maintenance and this became a standard for this type of tower.

Front Range

Description: Square pyramidal wooden

Location: Havre Boucher

Directions: From Havre Boucher, head east on Hwy 4 for 1.0 km and turn left on an unnamed road and the site is 350 meters

Coordinates: 45°40'54.4"N 61°31'37.6"W

Opened: 1879

Automated: 1963

Deactivated: Active

Height: 9 meters, 29 feet

Focal Height: 11 metes, 36 feet

Signal: Fixed green

Visitor Access: Grounds open, tower closed

Rear Range (image above)

Description: Square skeletal tower

Location: Havre Boucher

Coordinates: 45°40'40.8"N 61°31'42.6"W

Opened: 2010

Automated: 1963

Deactivated: Active

Height: 9 meters, 29 feet

Focal Height: 33 meters, 108 feet

Signal: Fixed green

Visitor Access: Grounds open, tower closed

Horton Bluff Range Front Lighthouse

In 1849 a petition was sent to the Nova Scotia House of Assembly calling for a lighthouse at the mouth of the Avon River. In 1851 the original Horton Bluff Range Front Lighthouse was opened. It was destroyed in a fire in 1883 and replaced that same year by Sydney S. Crowe and James Smith. The current lighthouse replaced it in 1961. It was automated in 1987 and deactivated in 2013.

Description: Square cylindrical concrete tower attached to corner of a fog signal building

Location: Avonport

Directions: From Avonport, head north on Oak Island Rd from NS-101 for 180 meters and turn right onto Bluff Rd. In 2.7 km turn left onto Lighthouse Rd and the site is 500 meters

Coordinates: 45°06'30.6"N 64°13'31.1"W

Opened: Original 1851, Second 1983, Current 1961

Automated: 1987

Deactivated: 2013

Height: 9 meters, 29 feet

Focal Height: 16 meters meters, 52 feet

Signal: Fixed green

Foghorn Signal: Blast every 30 seconds

Visitor Access: Grounds open, tower closed

Indian Harbour (Paddy's Head) Lighthouse

In 1901 the Indian Harbour Lighthouse opened on the south tip of Paddy's Head as a guide to ships using the entrance to Indian Harbour. The station was built by the Department of Marine. It was covered by vinyl which resembled wood.

Description: Square pyramidal wooden

Location: Indian Harbour

Directions: From Indian Head, head northwest on Paddys Head Rd for 1.4 km to find the site

Coordinates: 44°31'19.6"N 63°56'45.3"W

Opened: 1901

Automated: 1945

Deactivated: Active

Height: 10 meters, 33 feet

Focal Height: 11 meters, 36 feet

Signal: Fixed white

Foghorn signal: N/A

Visitor Access: Closed

Isaacs Harbour Lighthouse

The original Isaacs Harbour Lighthouse opened in 1874 as a guide to vessels travelling into the long inlet of Isaacs Harbour. J. T. Sinclair fulfilled the contract to build it. A hand foghorn was added to the site in 1900 and a 4th order Fresnel lens upgraded the lighting in 1910. The current lighthouse replaced the original in 1929 and it continues to be active. Isaac's Harbour Lighthouse was listed as a Heritage Lighthouse in 2018.

Description: Lantern on roof of square white dwelling

Location: Isaac's Harbour

Directions: From Isaacs Harbour, head southeast on Isaacs Harbour Rd for 1.9 km and find the site

Coordinates: 45°09'52.8"N 61°39'16.5"W

Opened: Original 1874, Current 1929

Automated: 1966

Deactivated: Active

Height: 35 meters, 116 feet

Focal Height: 42 meters, 139 feet

Signal: Fixes white

Foghorn Foghorn added 1900

Visitor Access: Grounds open, tower closed

Jeddore Rock Lighthouse

The original Jeddore Rock Lighthouse was erected in 1881 as an aid to ships travelling to Halifax Harbour. A 4th order Fresnel lens upgraded the lighting equipment in 1913. A hand fog horn was added in 1930. The site was automated in 1958 and remains active.

Description: Square skeletal tower

Location: Pleasant Point

Directions: Accessible by boat

Coordinates: 44°39'47.1"N 63°00'37.3"W

Opened: Original 1881, Current 2012

Automated: 1958

Deactivated: Active

Height: 15 meters, 49 feet

Focal Height: 29 meters, 96 feet

Signal: White flash every 10 seconds

Foghorn: Foghorn added 1930

Visitor Access: Closed

Jerome Point Lighthouse

The original Jerome Point Lighthouse opened in 1883 to guide vessels travelling to St. Peter's Canal which connected Bras d'Or Lake and the Atlantic Ocean. The construction was completed by Lawrence J. O'Toole. The current lighthouse and a new keeper's dwelling were opened in 1956. It continues to be active.

Description: Square pyramidal wooden tower

Location: St. Peter's

Directions: From St. Peter's, head west off Grenville St east of St. Peter's on an unnamed road for 1.2 km to find the site.

Coordinates: 45°38'53.9"N 60°52'21.8"W

Opened: Original 1883, Current 1956

Automated: 1958

Deactivated: Active

Height: 10.5 meters, 35 feet

Focal Height: 15.5 meters, 51 feet

Signal: Fixed red

Foghorn Signal: Fog alarm added 1884

Visitor Access: Grounds open, tower closed

Jerseyman Island Lighthouse

The original Jerseyman Island Lighthouse was built in 1872 as a guide to vessels using the northwest entrance to Arichat Harbour. F.S. Cunningham erected the tower and keeper's dwelling. A hand foghorn was an addition to the station in 1896. The current lighthouse was opened in 2017 and continues to be active.

Description: Square pyramidal wooden tower

Location: Arichat

Directions: Accessible by boat

Coordinates: 45°30'13.3"N 61°03'19.9"W

Opened: Original 1872, Current 2017

Automated: 1978

Deactivated: Active

Height: 7.5 meters, 25 feet

Focal Height: 12 meters, 39 feet

Signal: Fixed red

Foghorn: Fog alarm added 1896

Visitor Access: Grounds open, tower closed

Kidston Island Lighthouse

In 1875, the original Kidston Island Lighthouse opened as a guide to mariners travelling to Baddeck Harbour. Neil W. McKenzie was the contractor for the work. In 1909 the lighting equipment was updated with a 4th order Fresnel lens. The tower was restored in 2014.

Description: Square pyramidal wooden tower

Location: Baddeck

Directions: Accessible by boat

Coordinates: 46°05'53.3"N 60°44'31.3"W

Opened: 1875

Automated: 1960

Deactivated: Active

Height: 14.5 meters, 47 feet

Focal Height: 13.5 meters, 44 feet

Signal: Green flash every 12 seconds

Foghorn signal: N/A

Visitor Access: Grounds open, tower closed

L'Ardoise Harbor Range Lights

The L'Ardoise Harbor Range Lights were built in 1909 by L. Mury to guide ships to the entrance to safe anchrage at Lower L'Ardoise. The lights were deactivated in 1870. The rear range is in its original location where it is used as a storage shed while the front range has been relocated for private use.

Front Range (Image above)

Description: Square pyramidal wooden

Location: Port Michaud

Directions: From Gracieville, head east on Point Michaud Rd/NS-247 W for 2.1 km to find the site

Coordinates: 45°35'18.1"N 60°41'25.4"W

Opened: 1909

Automated: 1923

Deactivated: 1970

Height: 7 meters, 23 feet

Focal Height: Not known

Signal: Fixed red

Visitor Access: Closed

Rear Range

Description: Square pyramidal wooden

Location: St. Peter's

Coordinates: 45°35'48.8"N 60°44'35.0"W

Opened: 1909

Automated: 1923

Deactivated: 1970

Height: 7 meters, 23 feet

Focal Height: Not known

Signal: Fixed red

Visitor Access: Closed

Lockeport (Gull Rock) Lighthouse

The original Lockeport or Gull Rock Lighthouse opened in 1853 to guide ships to the entrance to Lockeport Harbour. A hand fog alarm was added in 1884 and in 1918 it was upgraded with a fog control building. The current lighthouse replaced the original in 1948. The fog-alarm building, workshop, and boathouse were removed when the station was automated in 1987.

Description: Square cylindrical tower

Location: Lockeport

Directions: Accessible by boat

Coordinates: 43°39'18.3"N 65°05'55.9"W

Opened: Original 1853, Current 1948

Automated: 1987

Deactivated: Active

Height: 13.5 meters, 44 feet

Focal Height: 17 meters, 56 feet

Signal: White flash every 15 seconds

Foghorn: Fog signal added 1918

Visitor Access: Grounds open, tower closed

Louisbourg Lighthouse

The original Louisburg Lighthouse opened in 1734. It was the 1st lighthouse to be built in Canada and the 2nd in North America. It was designed b Etienne Verrier and constructed by Francois Ganet. A fire destroyed the lantern room 2 years after it was opened and the light was out of service for 2 years. The lighthouse was destroyed in 1758 during a siege by the British. The 2nd lighthouse there opened in 1842 and it was lost in a 1922 fire. The current lighthouse opened in 1924 and continues to be active.

Description: Octagonal concrete tower

Location: Louisbourg

Directions: From Louisburg, head east on Havenside Rd for 500 meters, and turn right to stay on Havenside Rd. The site is 2.7 km from here

Coordinates: 45°54'24.0"N 59°57'30.5"W

Opened: Original 1734, Second 1842, Current 1924

Automated: 1989

Deactivated: Active

Height: 17 meters, 55 feet

Focal Height: 32 meters, 105 feet

Signal: White flash every 19 seconds

Foghorn Signal: Double blast every 2 minutes

Visitor Access: Grounds open, tower closed

Low Point Lighthouse

The original Low Point Lighthouse opened in 1832 to guide ships entering Sydney Harbour. In 1877 a larger lantern room was installed and in 1903 a fog alarm building was added. A 3rd order Fresnel lens updated the lighting in 1908. The octagonal, concrete tower opened in 1938, The light was automated in 1988 and the site is still active.

Description: Octagonal concrete tower

Location: Sydney

Directions: From New Victoria. head NW on Browns Rd for 650 meters and turn right onto Browns Rd/Browns Road Extension. In 650 meters, turn left onto Lighthouse Rd and the site is 550 meters.

Coordinates: 46°16'01.5"N 60°07'32.9"W

Opened: Original 1832, Current 1938

Automated: 1988

Deactivated: Active

Height: 22 meters, 72 feet

Focal Height: 26 meters, 85 feet

Signal: White flash every 5 seconds

Foghorn signal: 2 blasts every 60 seconds

Visitor Access: Grounds open, tower closed

Mabou Harbour Lighthouse

The original Mabou Harbour Lighthouse was part of a set of range lights opened in 1884 to guide ships into Mabou Harbour. They consisted of lanterns hung on a mast. They were replaced by wooden towers constructed by E.C. Embree in 1908. The front range tower was discontinued in 1987 and the rear range tower continues as the current Mabou Harbour Lighthouse. It was listed as a Recognized Federal Heritage Building in 2006.

Description: Square pyramidal wooden tower

Location: Mabou Harbour

Directions: From Mabou Harbour Mouth, head NW on Mabou Harbour Rd 300 meters and turn left on an unnamed road. The site is 350 meters.

Coordinates: 46°05'09.2"N 61°27'55.2"W

Opened: Original 1884, Current 1908

Automated: 1966

Deactivated: Active

Height: 14 meters, 47 feet

Focal Height: 14 meters, 46 feet

Signal: Fixed green

Foghorn signal: N/A

Visitor Access: Open (Serves as the Mabou Harbour Museum and Tourist Centre)

Marache Point Lighthouse

Petitions for a lighthouse to mark the entrances to Arichat Harbour were made in 1848 and local people provided a light in 1851. It was considered inferior by government inspectors and in 1869 a new lighthouse was built consisting of a dwelling with light rising from the roof. In 1909 the lighting was upgraded with a 5th order Fresnel lens. In 1949 the site was upgraded with a new tower, dwelling, storehouse and boathouse. When the station was automated in 1970, all the buildings except the tower were removed.

Description: Square pyramidal wooden tower

Location: Arichat

Directions: Head west on Cape Auguet Rd off Lobster Plant Road north of Cape Auguet and the site is 1.6 km

Coordinates: 45°28'50.3"N 61°02'04.6"W

Opened: Original 1851, Current 1949

Automated: 1970

Deactivated: Active

Height: 7 meters, 25 feet

Focal Height: 10 meters, 34 feet

Signal: Fixed white

Foghorn: Fog horn added 1896

Visitor Access: Grounds open, tower closed

Margaree Harbour Range Lights

Margaree Harbour sits at the mouth of Margaree River on the west coast of Cape Breton. A pier was built to improve access to the harbour which is shallow in portions. In 1900 the Margaree Harbour Range Lights were erected at the south side of the harbour with both showing fixed red signal. This was changed to fixed yellow at some point. The Margaree Harbour Front and Rear Range lighthouses were listed under the Heritage Lighthouse Protection Act in 2019.

Front Range

Description: Square pyramidal wooden

Location: Margaree Harbour

Directions: From Margaree Harbour. head west on Shore Rd/NS-219 W for 230 meters and turn right onto Margaree Harbour Village Rd where the site is 800 meters.

Coordinates: 46°26'22.6"N 61°06'45.1"W

Opened: 1900

Automated: 1963

Deactivated: Active

Height: 4.5 meters, 15 feet

Focal Height: 15 meters, 49 feet

Signal: Fixed yellow

Visitor Access: Closed

Rear range

Description: Square pyramidal wooden

Location: Margaree Harbour

Coordinates: 46°26'20.6"N 61°06'44.4"W

Opened: 1900

Automated: 1963

Deactivated: Active

Height: 6 meters, 20 feet

Focal Height: 21 meters, 68 feet

Signal: Fixed yellow

Visitor Access: Closed

Margaretsville Lighthouse

In 1856 Margaretsville residents requested a lighthouse be erected to mark the town wharf. The Margaretsville Lighthouse opened in 1859. It soon featured a black horizontal stripe as a daymark. A 4th order lens updated the lighting in 1915. The light was automated in 1963 and remains active.

Description: Square pyramidal wooden tower

Location: Margaretsville

Directions: 13 Lighthouse Rd, Margaretsville

Coordinates: 45°03'00.3"N 65°03'57.8"W

Opened: 1859

Automated: 1963

Deactivated: Active

Height: 7 meters, 22 feet

Focal Height: 9 meters, 30 feet

Signal: 2 white flashes every 20 seconds

Foghorn Signal: N/A

Visitor Access: Grounds open, tower open in summer

Maugher Beach (McNabs Island) Lighthouse

The quick red fox jumped over the lazy brown dog. The quick red fox jumped over the lazy brown dog. The quick red fox jumped over the lazy brown dog. The quick red fox jumped over the lazy brown dog. The quick red fox jumped over the lazy brown dog. The quick red fox jumped over the lazy brown dog. The quick red fox jumped over the lazy brown dog. The quick red fox jumped over the lazy brown dog. The quick red fox jumped over the lazy brown dog. The quick red fox jumped

Description: White, octagonal concrete tower

Location: Halifax

Directions: Accessible by boat

Coordinates: 44°36'07.9"N 63°32'01.0"W

Opened: Original 1828, Current 1941

Automated: 1983

Deactivated: Active

Height: 17.5 meters, 58 feet

Focal Height: 17 meters, 57 feet

Signal: Yellow flash every 30 seconds

Foghorn Signal: Blast every 25 seconds

Visitor Access: Grounds open, tower closed

McNeil Beach Lighthouse

The original McNeil Beach Lighthouse was erected in 1884 to aid ships entering the Great Bras d'Or Channel from Cabot Strait. It involved a beacon light of a lantern on a mast with a small shed on its base. The current lighthouse replaced it in 1909 when it was built by L. Mury. A fixed red signal was produced by a 6th order lens. When the Seal Island Bridge was completed in 1951 the lighthouse was deactivated.

Description: Square pyramidal wood tower

Location: Big Bras D"Or

Directions: Head south on Kempt Head Rd off NS-105 for 800 meters and turn right onto Kellys View Dr and after 500 meters, take trail coast and the site.

Coordinates: 46°13'43.2"N 60°29'25.1"W

Opened: Original 1884, Current 1909

Automated: 1962

Deactivated: 1965

Height: 10 meters, 33 feet

Focal Height: 9.5 meters, 31 feet

Signal: Fixed red

Foghorn signal: N/A

Visitor Access: Grounds open, tower closed

Medway Head Lighthouse

The original Medway Head Lighthouse opened in 1851 following local requests. The station included the attached keeper's dwelling, as well as an oil storage building and a boathouse. In 1927 a replacement tower was erected. In 1966 the 3rd lighthouse on the site was built, a fibreglass tower on a cement pad. The current tower opened in 1983 shortly before its automation 4 years later. The station continues to be active.

Description: Square pyramidal wood tower

Location: Port Medway

Directions: From Port Medway, head SW on Long Cove Rd for 4.5 km to find the site

Coordinates: 44°06'10.6"N 64°32'23.3"W

Opened: Original 1851, Second 1927, Third 1963, Current 1983

Automated: 1987

Deactivated: Active

Height: 8.5 meters, 28 feet

Focal Height: 24 meters, 79 feet

Signal: White flash every 12 seconds

Foghorn signal: N/A

Visitor Access: Grounds open, tower open during the summer

Merigomish Lighthouse

The Merigomish Lighthouse was opened in 1882 to guide ships travelling to Merigomish Harbour. It consisted of a square wooded tower with an attached dwelling. Currently the light is in private hands and in use as a residence.

Description: Square wood tower

Location: Kings Head

Directions: From Kings Head, head east on Little Harbour Rd for 2.4 km and turn right onto Levi White Rd. After 1.3 km take a slight left onto Lighthouse Rd for 500 meters and find the site

Coordinates: 45°39'06.4"N 62°28'45.4"W

Opened: 1882

Automated: N/A

Deactivated: 1897

Height: 10 meters, 33 feet

Focal Height: 32 meters, 105 feet

Signal: Fixed red

Foghorn Signal: N/A

Visitor Access: Closed

Mitchener Point Lighthouse

Due to mining of gypsum, the Avon River became busy with shipping of this ore in the 1800s. The Mitchener Point Lighthouse was built by Lawrence Mury in 1908 to help guide ships on the river. This tower was replaced by the current one in 1972. It was deactivated in 2001.

Description: Round fiberglass tower

Location: Hantsport

Directions: From Pembroke, head southeast on Nova Scotia Trunk 1 E for 950 meters and turn left onto Lighthouse Rd where the site is 400 meters

Coordinates: 45°02'38.0"N 64°08'47.0"W

Opened: Original 1908, Current 1972

Automated: 1993

Deactivated: 2001

Height: 10 meters, 33 feet

Focal Height: 15 meters, 49 feet

Signal: Fixed white

Foghorn Signal: N/A

Visitor Access: Closed

Mullins Point Rear Range Light

The Mullins Point Range Lights were erected to aid ships travelling to Wallace Harbour. The rear range light was erected in 1894 and became part of a set with the previously built Mullins Point Lighthouse. The contract was completed by Daniel McDonald. The lights became deactivated in 1965 and the Mullins Point Rear Range Light was sold into private hands. It was relocated and is used as a residence.

Description: Square pyramidal wood tower on keeper's dwelling

Location: Wallace

Directions: From Mullins Point, head south on Fox Harbour S Rd/N Wallace Rd for 900 meters and find the site

Coordinates: 45°49'27.6"N 63°26'36.3"W

Opened: 1894

Automated: 1963

Deactivated: 1965

Height: 14.5 meters, 48 feet

Focal Height: 12 meters, 39 feet

Signal: Fixed white

Foghorn Signal: N/A

Visitor Access: Closed

Munroe Point Lighthouse

The Munroe Point Lighthouse was built by P. L. Macfarlane in 1906 to guide ships into St. Ann's Bay. Munroe Point Lighthouse was automated in 1952 and then deactivated in 1962. The lighthouse was sold into private hands and is available for rental.

Description: White, square tower

Location: English Town

Directions: Accessible by boat

Coordinates: 46°15'20.6"N 60°35'30.6"W

Opened: 1906

Automated: 1952

Deactivated: 1962

Height: 10 meters, 32 feet

Focal Height: 20 meters, 67 feet

Signal: Fixed red

Foghorn Signal: N/A

Visitor Access: Closed

Neils' Harbour Lighthouse

The Neils' Harbour Lighthouse was opened in 1899 to aid vessels travelling into Neil's Harbour. The contract for building it was fulfilled by Mr. P. McFarlane. A foghorn was added to the station in 1910. Neil's Harbour Lighthouse was listed as a Heritage Lighthouse in 2015.

Description: Square pyramidal wood tower

Location: Neils Harbour

Directions: From Nells Harbour, head southeast on Lighthouse Rd off New Haven Road for 250 meters and the site

Coordinates: 46°48'23.3"N 60°19'11.0"W

Opened: 1899

Automated: 1956

Deactivated: Active

Height: 13 meters, 43 feet

Focal Height: 28 meters, 59 feet

Signal: Fixed white

Foghorn signal: N/A

Visitor Access: Grounds open, tower open in the summer

Outer Island Lighthouse

The Outer Island or Bon Portage Island Lighthouse was opened in 1964 to guide vessels into Barrington, West Bay and Shag Harbour. Henry Chute fulfilled the contract to build it. In 1915 the lighting was upgraded with a 4th order Fresnel lens. The current tower replaced the original in 1964 and the site continues to be active.

Description: Square cylindrical concrete tower

Location: Shag Harbour

Directions: Accessible by boat

Coordinates: 43°27'23.2"N 65°44'36.2"W

Opened: Original 1874, Current 1964

Automated: 1984

Deactivated: Active

Height: 12 meters, 40 feet

Focal Height: 14 meters, 46 feet

Signal: White flash every 10 seconds

Foghorn Signal: Blast every 20 seconds.

Visitor Access: Grounds open, tower closed

Parrsboro Lighthouse

The original Parrsboro Lighthouse opened in 1852 to guide mariners into the safety of Parrsboro Harbour. The tower was subject to bank erosion and in 1945 tilted to one side in the midst of a storm. The current tower was erected in 1980. It was automated in 1987 and continues to be active.

Description: Square cylindrical concrete tower attached to fog signal building

Location: Parrsboro

Directions: Take Lighthouse Road northeast from Whitehall Road for 450 meters and park at the end. Walk east to the breakwater and the site is at the tip

Coordinates: 45°23'14.6"N 64°18'56.2"W

Opened: Original 1852, Current 1980

Automated: 1987

Deactivated: Active

Height: 6.5 meters 21 feet

Focal Height: 8 meters, 26 feet

Signal: Fixed green

Foghorn Signal: Blast every 30 seconds

Visitor Access: Grounds open, tower closed

Peggy's Point (Peggy's Cove) Lighthouse

While it is officially known as the Peggys Point Lighthouse, it is more popularly called the Peggys Cove Lighthouse. It is certainly the best known and most photographed lighthouse in Canada. The original Peggys Point Lighthouse opened in 1868 to mark the entrance to St. Margaret's Bay. A 5th order lens upgraded the lighting in 1897 but it was destroyed in an explosion in the lantern room shortly thereafter. The current tower was built by Standard Construction Company and opened in 1915. It remains active.

Description: White, octagonal concrete tower

Location: Peggy's Cove

Directions: From NS 333 at Peggy's Cove, turn on Peggy's Point Road and continue to the end, where you will see the lighthouse

Coordinates: 44°29'30.8"N 63°55'08.0"W

Opened: Original 1868, Current 1915

Automated: 1958

Deactivated: Active

Height: 13 meters, 43 feet

Focal Height: 22 meters, 72 feet

Signal: Red flash every 5 seconds

Foghorn Signal: N/A

Visitor Access: Grounds open, tower closed

Peter Island Lighthouse

Requests for a lighthouse at the southern entrance of the Grand Passage between Brier Island and Long Island were made in the 1840s. The original Peter Island Lighthouse was opened in 1850 to cover this need. The current lighthouse was built in 1909 by W. Brooks. The Government of Canada listed Peter Island Lighthouse as a Heritage Lighthouse in 2021.

Description: Octagonal pyramidal wood tower

Location: Westport

Directions: Accessible only by boat

Coordinates: 44°15'26.4"N 66°20'15.3"W

Opened: Original 1850, Current 1909

Automated: 1984

Deactivated: 2014

Height: 12.5 meters, 41 feet

Focal Height: 19 meters, 62 feet

Signal: Yellow flash every 5 seconds

Foghorn Signal: 2 blasts every 20 seconds

Visitor Access: Closed

Pictou Customs House Lighthouse

In 1874 the Pictou Customs House was built in the town of Pictou. The Department of Marine noted that it aligned with Pictou Bar Lighthouse and received permission to mount a light from its tower. In 1954 wind destroyed the Customs House tower although a light was continued to be shone. The Pictou Bar Lighthouse burned in 2004.

Description: Tower of the Customs House

Location: Pictou

Directions: 38 Depot St, Pictou

Coordinates: 45°40'31.9"N 62°42'24.3"W

Opened: 1878

Automated: 1957

Deactivated: 1958

Height: Not known

Focal Height: 18 meters, 60 feet

Signal: Fixed red

Foghorn Signal: N/A

Visitor Access: Closed

Pictou Harbour Range Lights

The original Pictou Harbour Range Lights were lanterns on masts opened in 1889. They were built to show the channel between the sand spit off Pictou Bar Lighthouse on the south and Mudoch's Shoal on the North. In 1896 the current towers replaced these originals. The work was done by the Department of Marine after no satisfactory tenders were received. The towers were relocated to their current positions in 1908 by James Arbuckle. They were deactivated in 2012.

Front Range

Description: Square pyramidal wood

Location: Pictou

Directions: North side of the entrance to Pictou Harbour

Coordinates: 45°41'18.2"N 62°40'44.4"W

Opened: 1889

Automated: 1965

Deactivated: 2012

Height: 7 meters, 23 feet

Focal Height: 8 meters, 28 feet

Signal: Fixed red

Foghorn Signal: N/A

Visitor Access: Closed

Rear Range

Description: Square pyramidal wood

Location: Pictou

Coordinates: 45°41'18.2"N 62°40'47.1"W

Opened: 1889

Automated: 1965

Deactivated: 2012

Height: 11 meters, 38 feet

Focal Height: 17 meters, 56 feet

Signal: Fixed red

Foghorn Signal: N/A

Visitor Access: Closed

Port Bickerton Lighthouse

The original Port Bickerton Lighthouse was built by Emery Taylor and opened in 1901 as a harbour light for Port Bickerton. This was replaced in 1930 by a square dwelling with a lantern in its center. The current lighthouse opened in 1963 and the 1930 lighthouse was used as an interpretive centre. The site was automated in 1988 and remains active.

Description: White, square concrete tower

Location: Port Bickerton

Directions: From Port Bickerton, head east on E Side Bickerton Rd for 1.0 km and turn left on Lighthouse Rd where the site is 2.2 km

Coordinates: 45°05'24.0"N 61°42'01.7"W

Opened: Original 1901, Second 1930, Current 1963

Automated: 1988

Deactivated: Active

Height: 10 meters, 33 feet

Focal Height: 20.5 meters, 67 feet

Signal: White flash every 8 seconds

Foghorn: Foghorn added 1910

Visitor Access: Grounds open, tower closed

Port George Lighthouse

The Port George Harbour was created with a breakwater and pier and the Port George Lighthouse was erected to aid vessels entering it. 1909 the lighting was upgraded with a 6th order Fresnel lens. The lighthouse was moved to the shore in 1931. It was deactivated in 1999.

Description: Square pyramidal wood

Location: Port George

Directions: From Moshers Corner, head NE on Shore Rd E for 1.0 km and continue onto Shore Rd E. After 2.7 km, turn right onto Gates Mountain Rd and find the site.

Coordinates: 45°00'10.8"N 65°09'38.1"W

Opened: 1888

Automated: 1993

Deactivated: Active

Height: 7.5 meters, 25 feet

Focal Height: 9.5 meters, 31 feet

Signal: Fixed red

Foghorn Signal: N/A

Visitor Access: Grounds open, tower closed

Port Greville Lighthouse

In 1908 a pair of Range Lights were built by John D. Reid to aid ships entering Port Greville Harbour. After the front light was destroyed in 1940, the rear range became known as Port Greville Lighthouse and had a fixed white signal. The tower was deactivated in 1976 and moved near Sydney. It was moved back in 1998 and exhibited at the Age of Sail Heritage Centre.

Description: Square pyramidal wood

Location: Port Greville

Directions: From Port Greville, head NW on NS-209 NW for 1.1 km and find the site.

Coordinates: 45°24'54.7"N 64°33'08.5"W

Opened: 1908

Automated: 1960s

Deactivated: 1976

Height: 7.5 meters, 25 feet

Focal Height: 18 meters, 59 feet

Signal: Fixed white

Foghorn signal: N/A

Visitor Access: Grounds open, tower open late May to late September

Port Medway Lighthouse

The Port Medway Lighthouse was erected to guide mariners to the Port Medway Harbour. The tower was equipped with a 7th order lens. In 1979 the tower was covered in vinyl siding. The light was deactivated in 1989. In 2000 the Medway Area Communities Association promoted the establishment of a park with walkways, a pavilion and gardens

Description: Square pyramidal wood covered with viny

Location: Port Medway

Directions: From Port Medway, head northeast on Port Medway Rd for 220 meters and find the site

Coordinates: 44°07'55.5"N 64°34'28.4"W

Opened: 1989

Automated: 1959

Deactivated: 1989

Height: 8.5 meters, 28 feet

Focal Height: 9.5 meters, 31 feet

Signal: Fixed red

Foghorn Signal: N/A

Visitor Access: Grounds open, tower closed

Port Mouton Lighthouse

The original Port Mouton Lighthouse was built by G. S. Parker in 1873, as an aid to ships travelling to Port Mouton Harbour. In 1906 a foghorn was added to the site and in 1915, a fourth-order Fresnel lens upgraded the lighting equipment. The current lighthouse replaced the original in 1937. The tower was listed as a heritage lighthouse in 2015.

Description: Square pyramidal wood tower

Location: Port Mouton

Directions: Accessible by boat

Coordinates: 43°55'05.8"N 64°48'14.6"W

Opened: Original 1873, Current 1937

Automated: 1961

Deactivated: Active

Height: 5.5 meters, 18 feet

Focal Height: 17 meters, 55 feet

Signal: White flash every6 12 seconds

Foghorn: Foghorn added 1906

Visitor Access: Grounds open, tower closed

Prim Point Lighthouse

A petition for a lighthouse at the entrance of Digby Gut was made in 1801 and the original station was opened in 1804. It was destroyed in an 1808 fire and the second Prim Point Lighthouse opened in 1817. A steam whistle for fog control was added in 1871. In 1873 the second tower was also destroyed by fire. Prim Point Lighthouse was listed as a Heritage Lighthouse in 2015.

Description: Square cylindrical concrete tower attached to fog signal building

Location: Digby

Directions: From Bay View, head east on Broadcove Rd for 500 meters and turn left onto Lighthouse Rd. You will find the site in 1.0 km.

Coordinates: 44°41'25.9"N 65°47'04.2"W

Opened: Original 1804, Second 1875, Current 1964

Automated: 1987

Deactivated: Active

Height: 14 meters, 46 feet

Focal Height: 25 meters, 82 feet

Signal: White flash every 6 seconds

Foghorn signal: Blast every 30 seconds.

Visitor Access: Grounds open, tower closed

Pubnico Harbour Lighthouse

The original Pubnico Harbour Lighthouse opened in 1854 as a guide to ships entering Pubnico Harbour. An addition to the dwelling was made in 1858 which would be welcomed by the keeper and his family of eight. The tower was raised ten feet in 1889 and a 6th order Fresnel lens upgraded the lighting. The light was deactivated in 2000 but reactivated in 2005.

Description: Conical fiberglass tower

Location: Pubnico

Directions: From Lower East Pubnico, head south on Nova Scotia Trunk 3 E for 3.9 km and turn right onto Lighthouse Rd where the light is a short distance.

Coordinates: 43°35'53.4"N 65°46'55.6"W

Opened: Original 1854, Second 1889, Current 1984

Automated: 1987

Deactivated: Active

Height: 11 meters, 36 feet

Focal Height: 12 meters, 40 feet

Signal: Red flash every 3 seconds

Foghorn: Hand-operated foghorn added in 1898

Visitor Access: Grounds open, tower closed

Queensport (Rook Island) Lighthouse

The original Queensport (Rook Island) Lighthouse opened in 1882 as a guide to ships entering Queensport Harbour. It was built by James McDonald on Rook Island. A hand-operated foghorn was added to the station in 1900. The current lighthouse replaced the original in 1936. The site was automated in 1955 and the foghorn was deactivated. Queensport Lighthouse was placed on the Canadian Register of Historic Places in 2005.

Description: Tower on roof of square white dwelling

Location: Queensport

Directions: Accessible by boat

Coordinates: 45°20'52.6"N 61°16'18.9"W

Opened: Original 1882, Current 1936

Automated: 1955

Deactivated: Active

Height: 12.5 meters, 41 feet

Focal Height: 16.5 meters, 54 feet

Signal: White flash every 4 seconds

Foghorn Signal: Hand-operated foghorn added 1900

Visitor Access: Grounds open, tower closed

River Bourgeois Lighthouse

The original River Bourgeois Lighthouse was built by Edward Doyle and opened in 1903. It was erected to mark the entrance to Bourgeois Inlet. By 1962 the tower was in poor shape and the lantern was removed. In 1989 the lighthouse was burned by the Coast Guard as it was deemed unsafe. The local community built the current tower as a replica of the original and the Coast provided a light for it.

Description: Square pyramidal wood tower

Location: River Bourgeois

Directions: From River Bourgeois, head west on Church Point Rd for 1.0 km and walk 200 meters to coast to see the site.

Coordinates: 45°37'32.8"N 60°56'51.1"W

Opened: Original 1903, Current replica 2003

Automated: 1993

Deactivated: Active privately

Height: 7.5 meters, 25 feet

Focal Height: N/A

Signal: Fixed red

Foghorn Signal: N/A

Visitor Access: Grounds open, tower closed

Sable Island Range Lights

Sable Island lies far off the Nova Scotia mainland and the sandbars and reefs have seen over 300 vessels wrecked there. The original Sable Island Range Lights were erected in 1873 to guide ships through this dangerous passage. In 1934 the East End tower was destroyed in a fire caused by lightning and a square, pyramidal tower replaced it 1935. By 1973 erosion had endangered this light and the current tower was opened. Both lights are inactive.

East End (Image above)

Description: Square steel tower

Location: Canso

Directions: Accessible by boat

Coordinates: 43°57'36.2"N 59°47'26.2"W

Opened: 1975

Automated: 1960

Deactivated: 2012

Height: 18 meters, 59 feet

Focal Height: 36 meters, 118 feet

Signal: White flash every 10 seconds

Foghorn: Fog whistle 1870

Visitor Access: Grounds open, tower closed

West End

Description: Square steel tower

Location: Canso

Directions: Accessible by boat

Coordinates: 43°55'55.1"N 60°01'22.0"W

Opened: 1980

Automated: 1960

Deactivated: 2004

Height: 26 meters, 85 feet

Focal Height: 32 meters, 105 feet

Signal: White flash every 10 seconds

Foghorn: Fog whistle 1870

Visitor Access: Grounds open, tower closed

Salmon River Lighthouse

The Salmon River Lighthouse was built on the Salmon River Wharf. A fog bell was included at the site. After the light was discontinued in the 1980s, it was sold into private hands and relocated to West Pubnico. It has been painted as an Acadian Flag and attached to a craft shop

Description: White, square pyramidal

Location: Pubnico

Directions: 363 NS-335, West Pubnico

Coordinates: 43°41'21.4"N 65°47'42.2"W

Opened: 1924

Automated: Not known

Deactivated: 1980s

Height: 8.5 meters, 28 feet

Focal Height: Not known

Signal: Fixed white

Foghorn Signal: Fog Bell 1 stroke every 6 seconds

Visitor Access: Grounds open, tower closed

Sambro Harbour Lighthouse

Sambro Harbour is fairly small and affords safe anchorage for small vessels. In 1899 the Sambro Harbour Lighthouse was built to guide ships entering the harbour. It was erected by the Department of Marine and Fisheries. In 2016 the lighthouse was demolished as it was in poor condition. A slightly larger tower in the same salt shaker style replaced it.

Description: White, square pyramidal

Location: Sambro

Directions: From Sambro, head south on Bull Point Rd/Old Sambro Rd/NS-349 S for 1.0 km and find the site

Coordinates: 44°28'30.3"N 63°35'45.3"W

Opened: Original 1899, Current 2016

Automated: 1961

Deactivated: Active

Height: 10 meters, 33 feet

Focal Height: 10.5 meters, 34 feet

Signal: Fixed green

Foghorn signal: N/A

Visitor Access: Closed

Sambro Island Lighthouse

The Sambro Island Lighthouse, which opened in 1758, is the oldest lighthouse still in operation in the Americas. This came about after the British destroyed the Louisbourg Lighthouse in 1758 and the Boston Harbour Lighthouse in 1776. A fog alarm was added to the site in 1865. In 1877 a 2nd order Fresnel lens upgraded the lighting equipment and in 1906 it was upgraded with a 1st order Fresnel lens. After a 2007 storm destroyed the submarine cable, the site was installed with solar panels. The station was listed as a Heritage Place in 1996.

Description: Octagonal stone tower

Location: Sambro

Directions: Accessible by boat

Coordinates: 44°26'12.1"N 63°33'47.9"W

Opened: 1780

Automated: 1988

Deactivated: Active

Height: 25 meters, 82 feet

Focal Height: 43 meters, 142 feet

Signal: White flash every 5 seconds

Foghorn signal: 3 blasts every 60 seconds

Visitor Access: Closed

Sandy Point Lighthouse

The original Sandy Point Lighthouse was built by George De Champ and opened in 1873 to guide ships to Shelburne Harbour. However the lighthouse was destroyed in a fire only 5 years later. A replacement was erected by George De Champ which opened in 1880. A 4th order Fresnel lens upgraded the lighting in 1914. The site was deactivated in 1996. Major restoration work was completed in 2008 and the light was reactivated and operated privately.

Description: White, square pyramidal

Location: Shelburne

Directions: From Sandy Point, head south on Lighthouse Rte/Sandy Point Rd for 850 meters and the site is on the right

Coordinates: 43°41'29.3"N 65°19'31.3"W

Opened: Original 1873, Current 1880

Automated: 1980

Deactivated: Active, privately maintained

Height: 9 meters, 39 feet

Focal Height: 14 meters, 47 feet

Signal: Fixed red

Foghorn signal: N/A

Visitor Access: Grounds open, tower closed

Schafner Point Lighthouse

The Schafner Point Lighthouse was opened in 1885 to guide vessels travelling the entrance to the Annapolis River. The work was completed by John Wagstaff. A stone wall was built two years later as protection against erosion. The site was automated in 1993 and remains active. Some restoration work was done in 2023.

Description: White, square pyramidal

Location: Port Royal

Directions: From Port Royal, head southwest on Granville Rd for 1.5 km to find the site.

Coordinates: 44°42'35.5"N 65°37'08.6"W

Opened: 1885

Automated: 1993

Deactivated: Active

Height: 11 meters, 36 feet

Focal Height: 13 meters, 43 feet

Signal: Fixed white

Foghorn signal: N/A

Visitor Access: Grounds open, tower closed

Seal Island Light Museum

In 1977 there were plans to move the lantern room and lens from the Seal Island Lighthouse to the National Museum of Science and Technology in Ottawa. Local residents protested this and the next year it was decided to keep that equipment in Barrington. A half size replica of Seal Island Lighthouse was built to house it in 1985.

Description: Octagonal wood tower

Location: Barrington

Directions: 2422 Nova Scotia Trunk 3, Barrington

Coordinates: 43°34'00.6"N 65°34'50.6"W

Opened: 1985

Automated: 1985

Deactivated: N/A

Height: 11 meters, 35 feet

Focal Height: N/A

Signal: N/A

Foghorn signal: N/A

Visitor Access: Open daily mid June to mid September

Seal Island Lighthouse

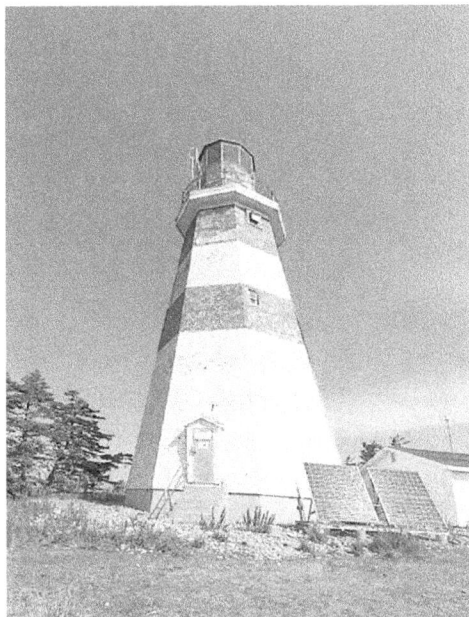

The Seal Island Lighthouse was erected in 1831 to aid ships travelling to and from the Bay of Fundy. It was built by Tidmarsh and Sargent of Nova Scotia and Barlow and Ward of New Brunswick and was the 8th lighthouse built by Nova Scotia and is the 2nd oldest surviving. A fog bell was added to the site in 1832. A 2nd order Fresnel lens upgraded the lighting equipment in 1870.

Description: Octagonal wood tower

Location: Clark's Harbour

Directions: Accessible by boat

Coordinates: 43°23'40.0"N 66°00'51.0"W

Opened: 1831

Automated: 1990

Deactivated: Active

Height: 21 meters, 68 feet

Focal Height: 31 meters, 102 feet

Signal: White flash every 10 seconds

Foghorn signal: 3 blasts every 60 seconds

Visitor Access: Grounds open, tower closed

Sheet Harbour Passage Range Lights

The Sheet Harbour Passage Range Lights were built by A. Balcon in 1915 as a guide to ships travelling the Sheet Harbour Passage between Sober Island and the mainland. The lights were automated in 1993 and continue to be active.

Front Range

Description: White, square pyramidal

Location: Sheet Harbour Passage

Directions: From Sheet Harbour, head southeast on Passage Rd for 1.6 km and the site is on the left

Coordinates: 44°51'30.0"N 62°26'56.0"W

Opened: 1915

Automated: 1993

Deactivated: Active

Height: 8 meters, 27 feet

Focal Height: 16 meters, 52 feet

Signal: Fixed white

Visitor Access: Grounds open, tower closed

Rear Range (Image above)

Description: White, square pyramidal

Location: Sheet Harbour Passage

Coordinates: 44°51'30.0"N 62°26'56.0"W

Opened: 1915

Automated: 1993

Deactivated: Active

Height: 9 meters, 29 feet

Focal Height: 20 meters, 65 feet

Signal: Fixed white

Visitor Access: Grounds open, tower closed

Sheet Rock Lighthouse

The original Sheet Rock Lighthouse was built by R. Rutledge and D. Drake in 1879 to guide ships to Sheet Harbour. In 1883 a landing was built but was often in need of repairs due to its exposed location. In 1936 a new lighthouse was built to replace the original tower The current lighthouse was opened in 1980, at which time the 1936 tower was destroyed. It continues to be active.

Description: Round fiberglass tower

Location: Sheet Harbour Passage

Directions: Accessible by boat

Coordinates: 44°49'50.4"N 62°29'30.6"W

Opened: Original 1879, Current 1980

Automated: 1968

Deactivated: Active

Height: 8 meters, 30 feet

Focal Height: 23.5 meters, 77 feet

Signal: White flash every 4 seconds

Foghorn: Hand-operated foghorn added 1909

Visitor Access: Grounds open, tower closed

Spencers Island Lighthouse

Spencers Island is located near the Minas Channel which connects Minas Basin and the Bay of Fundy. For many years it was a major ship building area. The Spencers Island Lighthouse opened in 1904 to guide vessels through this channel. After being discontinued in 1987 it was acquired from the government by a local community group and used as a museum. Restoration was done in 1996.

Description: White, square pyramidal

Location: Spencers Island

Directions: From Spencers Island, head east on Spencers Island Rd for 200 meters and turn right onto Spencers Beach Rd and the site

Coordinates: 45°21'17.5"N 64°42'37.3"W

Opened: 1904

Automated: 1988

Deactivated: 1987, reactivated privately 2006

Height: 10 meters, 33 feet

Focal Height: 10.5 meters, 34 feet

Signal: Fixed white

Foghorn: Fog bell added in 1920

Visitor Access: Grounds open, tower open daily except Monday in July and August

Spry Bay Lighthouse

The Spry Bay Lighthouse was originally part of a set of range lights opened in 1916 as a guide to ships entering Spry Bay. The work was done by the Standard Construction Company. In 1987 the rear light was discontinued and the front light became a sector light showing red, white and green with the white showing the correct path. The light became inactive in 2020.

Description: Square wood tower

Location: Spry Bay

Directions: From Spry Bay, head southwest on Nova Scotia Trunk 7 W for 1.3 km and turn left onto Boutiliers Settlement Rd. After 2.3 km park and walk 0.5 km to the coast and the site

Coordinates: 44°49'21.5"N 62°35'54.3"W

Opened: 1916

Automated: 1993

Deactivated: 2020

Height: 7.5 meters, 25 feet

Focal Height: 22.5 meters, 74 feet

Signal: Fixed white

Foghorn signal: N/A

Visitor Access: Grounds open, tower closed

St. Paul Island Range Lights

St. Paul Island has been a dangerous obstruction to passing ships for many years. In 1839 the St. Paul Island Range Lights were built to aid mariners through the area. In 1872 a steam fog whistle was built after shipwrecks due to fog. In 1914 a fire destroyed the South Point Tower and a metal tower was built to replace it in 1916. The current tower replaced it in 1964. The South Point Tower was moved to Dingwall in 2011 to the St. Paul Island Museum.

North Point (Image above)

Description: Octagonal concrete tower

Location: Cape North

Directions: Accessible by boat

Coordinates: 47°13'36.0"N 60°08'24.3"W

Opened: Original 1839, Current 1962

Automated: 1991

Deactivated: 2015

Height: 14 meters, 46 feet

Focal Height: 38 meters, 126 feet

Signal: Fixed white

Foghorn Signal: 2 blast every 60 seconds

Visitor Access: Grounds open, tower closed

South Point

Description: Round fiberglass tower

Location: Dingwall

Directions: From Dingwall, head SW on Mountainview Rd for 200 meters and turn left onto Dingwall Rd and the site is 800 meters

Coordinates: 46°54'02.6"N 60°27'40.0"W

Opened: Original 1831, Current 1964

Automated: 1964

Deactivated: 2015

Height: 6 meters, 20 feet

Focal Height: 46 meters 150 feet

Signal: 4 white flashes every 12 seconds

Foghorn Signal: 2 blast every 60 seconds

Visitor Access: Grounds open, tower closed

Sydney Range Lights

Sydney Harbour have the Northwest Bar and Southeast Bar restricting the safe access. The original Sydney Range Lights were opened in 1905 to aid ships travelling there. The towers were built by P. L. McFarlane. In 1965 both towers were automated. The rear tower was replaced by a skeletal mast in 2009. The front tower was replaced by the current lighthouse in 2010.

Front Range (Image above)

Description: Octagonal pyramidal wood

Location: Sydney

Directions: From Edwardsville, head NW on Point Edward Hwy for 1.8 km and turn right on an unnamed road to find the site

Coordinates: 46°10'48.2"N 60°15'01.1"W

Opened: Original 1905, Current 2010

Automated: 1965

Deactivated: Active

Height: 17.5 meters, 58 feet

Focal Height: 18 meters, 60 feet

Signal: Yellow flash every 4 seconds

Visitor Access: Closed

Rear Range

Description: Triangular skeletal mast

Location: Sydney

Coordinates: 46°10'27.9"N 60°15'20.3"W

Opened: Original 1905, Current 2009

Automated: 1965

Deactivated: Active

Height: 9.5 meters, 311 feet

Focal Height: 37 meters, 121 feet

Signal: Yellow flash every 4 seconds

Visitor Access: Closed

Terence Bay Lighthouse

The original Terence Bay Light was a lantern on a mast opened in 1885 b Patrick A. Fahey to mark the west side of the entrance to Terence Bay. In 1903 the site was updated with a wooden tower erected with government day labour. The light was automated in 1957. The Terence Bay Lighthouse Committee was granted ownership of the lighthouse in 2016 and is in the process of insuring site access. Terence Bay Lighthouse was listed as a Heritage Lighthouse in 2015.

Description: Square pyramidal wood tower

Location: Terence Bay Lighthouse

Directions: From Sandy Cove, head SE on Sandy Cove Rd for 300 meters and turn right onto Leo Ln to see the site.

Coordinates: 44°27'36.6"N 63°42'20.8"W

Opened: Original 1885, Current 1903

Automated: 1957

Deactivated: Active

Height: 8 meters, 26 feet

Focal Height: 14.5 meters, 48 feet

Signal: Fixed red

Foghorn Signal: N/A

Visitor Access: Grounds open, tower closed

Trenton Range Lights

The original Trenton Range Lights were automated pole lights erected to guide ships into Pictou Harbour. A wooden pyramidal tower replaced the front range in 1962 and a steel skeleton tower replaced the rear. Both were deactivated in 2018.

Front Range (Image above)

Description: Square pyramidal tower

Location: Trenton

Directions: From Trenton, head west on Trenton Connector for 800 meters and the site is on the left

Coordinates: 45°37'25.9"N 62°38'53.8"W

Opened: Original 1920, Current 1952

Automated: 1920

Deactivated: 2018

Height: 4.5 meters, 15 feet

Focal Height: 18 meters, 60 feet

Signal: Fixed red

Visitor Access: Grounds open, tower closed

Rear Range

Description: Skeleton tower

Location: Trenton

Coordinates: 45°37'11.4"N 62°38'15.3"W

Opened: Original 1920, Current 1952

Automated: 1920

Deactivated: 2018

Height: Not known

Focal Height: Not known

Signal: Fixed red

Visitor Access: Grounds open, tower closed

Victoria Beach Lighthouse

The Victoria Beach Lighthouse was built by John Roney and opened in 1901. It was erected to guide ships through the Digby Gut. It was listed as a Heritage Lighthouse in 2015 and was deactivated that same year.

Description: White, square pyramidal tower

Location: Victoria Beach

Directions: From Port Wade, head SW on Granville Rd for 4.3 km. Turn left onto Victoria Beach Rd and the site.

Coordinates: 44°40'33.6"N 65°45'12.5"W

Opened: 1901

Automated: Not known

Deactivated: 2015

Height: 8 meters, 26 feet

Focal Height: 16 meters, 52 feet

Signal: Fixed white

Foghorn Signal: N/A

Visitor Access: Grounds open, tower closed

Walton Harbour Lighthouse

The Walton Harbour Lighthouse opened in 1872 to mark the harbour at the mouth of the Walton River. Timothy Parker built the lighthouse and became its first keeper. A 4th order Fresnel lens upgraded the lighting in 1915. After its deactivation, local volunteers maintained the tower and in 1992 is was listed as a Heritage Lighthouse.

Description: White, square pyramidal tower

Location: Walton

Directions: From Walton, head northwest on Hibbert Weir Rd for 800 meters and find the site

Coordinates: 45°14'03.2"N 64°00'42.9"W

Opened: 1872

Automated: 1970

Deactivated: 1978

Height: 8.5 meters, 38 feet

Focal Height: 18 meters, 60 feet

Signal: 2 white flash every 14 seconds

Foghorn signal: N/A

Visitor Access: Grounds open, tower open mid-May to mid-October

Wallace Harbour Range Lights

The Wallace Harbour Range Lights were erected by John D. Reid in 1904 to guide ships into Wallace Harbour between Palmer Point and Caulfield Point. The front range light was changed to a sector light in 1990 and is still active. The rear range light was sold to private hands in 1994 and it was relocated to its current location.

Front Range (Image above)

Description: White, square pyramidal tower

Location: Wallace

Directions: From Wallace, head east on NS-6 E for 400 meters and the site is on the left.

Coordinates: 45°48'47.2"N 63°27'43.1"W

Opened: 1904

Automated: 1958

Deactivated: Active

Height: 8.5 meters, 28 feet

Focal Height: 12.5 meters, 41 feet

Signal: Fixed red

Foghorn signal: N/A

Visitor Access: Grounds open, tower closed

Rear Range

Description: White, square pyramidal tower

Location: Malagash Mine

Coordinates: 45°48'32.0"N 63°17'23.2"W

Opened: 1904

Automated: 1958

Deactivated: 1990

Height: 8.5 meters, 28 feet

Focal Height: 30 meters, 100 feet

Signal: Fixed red

Foghorn signal: N/A

Visitor Access: Closed

West Head Lighthouse

The original West Head Lighthouse opened in 1888 to guide ships to the western entrance to Barrington Passage. It had been moved from Liverpool Bay. The lens from this original light is displayed in the Archelaus Smith Museum in Centreville, Cape Sable Island. The current tower opened in 1972 and continues to be active.

Description: Cylindrical fiberglass tower with 2 horizontal bands

Location: Clark's Harbour

Directions: From Clark's Harbour, head west on Hwy 330/Main St/NS-330 N for 1.5 km and turn left onto Boundry St where the site is 450 meters

Coordinates: 43°27'23.8"N 65°39'16.9"W

Opened: Original 1888, Current 1972

Automated: 1972

Deactivated: Active

Height: 6 meters, 20 feet

Focal Height: 15.5 meters, 51 feet

Signal: Fixed red

Foghorn signal: 2 blasts every 60 seconds

Visitor Access: Grounds open, tower closed

Western Head Lighthouse

The station on Western Head began as a fog control site in 1924. The lighthouse was not built until 1962 when it was erected to mark the western entrance to Liverpool Bay. In 1988 the lighthouse was automated and remains active today.

Description: Octagonal concrete tower

Location: Liverpool

Directions: From Western Head, head southeast on Breakwater Rd for 650 meters to find the site.

Coordinates: 43°59'20.8"N 64°39'44.5"W

Opened: 1962

Automated: 1988

Deactivated: Active

Height: 14 meters, 46 feet

Focal Height: 17 meters, 56 feet

Signal: White flash every 15 seconds

Foghorn signal: Blast every 60 seconds

Visitor Access: Grounds open, tower closed

Westhaver Island Lighthouse

In 1882 the original Westhaver Island Lighthouse was erected by James Smith to aid mariners travelling to Mahone Bay. The lighthouse was destroyed in a fire in 1887 and a lantern was shone from a mast to send a signal. The current tower was built in 1985 and was automated. The light continues to be active.

Description: Round fiberglass tower

Location: Mahone Bay

Directions: From Maders Cove, head northeast on Kinburn Acres Rd for 500 meters and the lighthouse can be seen off the coast on Westhaver Island

Coordinates: 44°26'09.8"N 64°20'15.3"W

Opened: Original 1882, Current 1985

Automated: 1985

Deactivated: Active

Height: 7.5 meters, 25 feet

Focal Height: 9.5 meters, 31 feet

Signal: White flash every 4 seconds

Foghorn Signal: N/A

Visitor Access: Grounds open, tower closed

Whitehead Island (Whitehaven Harbour) Lighthouse

The original Whitehead Island Lighthouse was erected on 1854 as a guide to ships travelling the southern coast of Nova Scotia. Substantial improvements were made in 1874 including renewing the lighting, adding a story to the tower and building an oil storage building. In 1913 a new fog alarm building and dwelling were added. The current tower was built in 1978 and is still active.

Description: Square cylindrical tower

Location: Pubnico

Directions: Accessible by boat

Coordinates: 43°39'45.8"N 65°52'02.6"W

Opened: Original 1874, Second 1934, Third 1967, Current 1978

Automated: 1998

Deactivated: 2018

Height: 9 meters, 30 feet

Focal Height: 18 meters, 60 feet

Signal: White flash every 60 seconds

Foghorn signal: Blast every 30 seconds

Visitor Access: Grounds open, tower closed

Woods Harbour Lighthouse

The original Woods Harbour Lighthouse was built in 1900 to protect ships from Big Ledge where it is situated. It also marks the southern entrance to Cockerwit Passage and of Lower Woods Harbour. A hand fog horn was included with the station. The current lighthouse was opened in 1963 and remains active.

Description: White square tower

Location: Lower Woods Harbour

Directions: Accessible by boat

Coordinates: 43°31'10.5"N 65°44'43.1"W

Opened: Original 1900, Current 1963

Automated: 1963

Deactivated: Active

Height: 6.5 meters, 21 feet

Focal Height: 6.5 meters, 21 feet

Signal: White flash every 5 seconds

Foghorn Signal: Blast every 30 seconds

Visitor Access: Closed

Woody Point (Barnes Point) Lighthouse

The Woody Point Lighthouse was originally built in 1911 at Woody Point or Barnes Point in New Brunswick by John A. Lea. The light was deactivated in 1976 and sold into private hands. It was moved to its present location where the owner integrated into a summer residence.

Description: Square pyramidal wood tower

Location: Amherst Shore

Directions: From Amherst Shore, head NE on Aggermore Point Rd from NS-366 for 200 meters and the lighthouse is on the right.

Coordinates: 45°57'51.9"N 63°52'53.2"W

Opened: 1911

Automated: Not known

Deactivated: 1976

Height: 11 meters, 32 feet

Focal Height: 12 meters, 40 feet

Signal: Fixed white

Foghorn Signal: N/A

Visitor Access: Closed

Other lighthouses1

Name: Beaver Island   **Location:** Beaver Harbourbel
Opened: 1985   **Access:** Grounds open, tower closed
Coordinates: 44°49'29.2"N 62°20'16.0"W

Name: Bon Portage   **Location:** Outer Island
Opened: 1964   **Access:** Grounds open, tower closed
Coordinates: 43°27'23.2"N 65°44'36.2"W

Name: Cameron Island   **Location:** Cameron Island
Opened: 1977   **Access:** Grounds open, tower closed
Coordinates: 45°48'55.4"N 61°00'27.7"W

Name: Candlebox Island   **Location:** Wedgeport
Opened: 1963   **Access:** Grounds open, tower closed
Coordinates: 43°39'44.6"N 66°02'43.3"W

Name: Cape Negro Island   **Location:** Cape Negro
Opened: 1915   **Access:** Accessible by boat
Coordinates: 43°30'26.2"N 65°20'44.2"W

Name: Ciboux Island   **Location:** Big Bras D'Or
Opened: 1980   **Access:** Grounds open, tower closed
Coordinates: 46°23'06.4"N 60°22'25.8"W

Name: Country Island   **Location:** Seal Harbour
Opened: 1968   **Access:** Closed
Coordinates: 45°05'59.8"N 61°32'31.9"W

Name: Digby Gut   **Location:** Digby
Opened: 1963   **Access:** Closed
Coordinates: 44°41'17.1"N 65°45'34.6"W

Name: Egg Island   **Location:** Clam Harbour
Opened: 1962   **Access:** Closed
Coordinates: 44°39'52.7"N 62°51'48.4"W

Name: Green Island   **Location:** Cape Breton
Opened: 1987   **Access:** Grounds open, tower closed
Coordinates: 45°28'41.3"N 60°53'57.6"W

Name: Gregory Island   **Location:** French Cove
Opened: 2013   **Access:** Grounds open, tower closed
Coordinates: 45°42'38.5"N 60°48'01.3"W

Other lighthouses2

Name: Guysborough (Harbour)   **Location**: Guysborough
Opened: 1982   **Access**: Closed
Coordinates: 45°22'39.9"N 61°29'26.7"W

Name: Henry Island   **Location**: Port Hood
Opened: 1902   **Access**: Grounds and tower opened occasionally
Coordinates: 45°58'37.6"N 61°35'59.4"W

Name: Kaulbach Island Range   **Location**: Mahone Bay
Opened: 1914   **Access**: Grounds open, tower closed
Coordinates: 44°28'11.3"N 64°16'53.3"W

Name: Kidston Island West End **Location**: Baddeck
Opened: 1976   **Access**: Grounds open, tower closed
Coordinates: 46°05'33.2"N 60°45'00.7"W

Name: Liscomb Island   **Location**: Liscomb
Opened: 1921   **Access**: Grounds open, tower closed
Coordinates: 44°59'15.8"N 61°57'58.4"W

Name: Main-A-Dieu   **Location**: Main-A-Dieu
Opened: 1979   **Access**: Grounds open, tower closed
Coordinates: 46°00'13.6"N 59°47'41.0"W

Name: Margaree Island   **Location**: Margaree Harbour
Opened: 1858   **Access**: Grounds open, tower closed
Coordinates: 46°21'26.8"N 61°15'47.4"W

Name: Mosher Island   **Location**: LaHave
Opened: 1989   **Access**: Grounds open, tower closed
Coordinates: 44°14'14.6"N 64°18'59.1"W

Name: Pearl Island (Green I.) **Location**: Mahone Bay
Opened: 1874   **Access**: Grounds open, tower closed
Coordinates: 44°22'57.2"N 64°02'54.0"W

Name: Pease Island   **Location**: Wedgeport
Opened: 1992   **Access**: Grounds open, tower closed
Coordinates: 43°37'42.6"N 66°01'34.9"W

Name: Pictou Island South End **Location**: Pictou
Opened: 1974   **Access**: Grounds open, tower closed
Coordinates: 45°48'14.2"N 62°35'11.7"W

Other lighthouses3

Name: Pomquet Island   **Location**: Bayfield
Opened: 1868   **Access**: Grounds open, tower closed
Coordinates: 45°39'27.5"N 61°44'50.6"W

Name: Quaker Island   **Location**: Chester
Opened: 1981   **Access**: Grounds open, tower closed
Coordinates: 44°30'53.7"N 64°13'57.2"W

Name: Scatarie   **Location**: Scaterie Island
Opened: 1981   **Access**: Grounds open, tower closed
Coordinates: 46°02'04.3"N 59°40'33.7"W

Name: Stoddart Island   **Location**: Shag Harbour
Opened: 1886   **Access**: Closed
Coordinates: 43°28'35.2"N 65°43'10.7"W

Name: Sydney Bar   **Location**: Sydney
Opened: 1948   **Access**: Closed
Coordinates: 46°12'20.7"N 60°13'07.1"W

Name: The Salvages   **Location**: Blanche
Opened: 1965   **Access**: Grounds open, tower closed
Coordinates: 43°28'08.1"N 65°22'44.0"W

Name: Tusket River   **Location**: Wedgeport
Opened: 1962   **Access**: Grounds open, tower closed
Coordinates: 43°42'12.6"N 65°57'05.9"W

Name: White Head Island   **Location**: Lower Whitehead
Opened: 1951   **Access**: Grounds open, tower closed
Coordinates: 45°11'49.1"N 61°08'10.8"W

Tours

Cape Breton Tour1

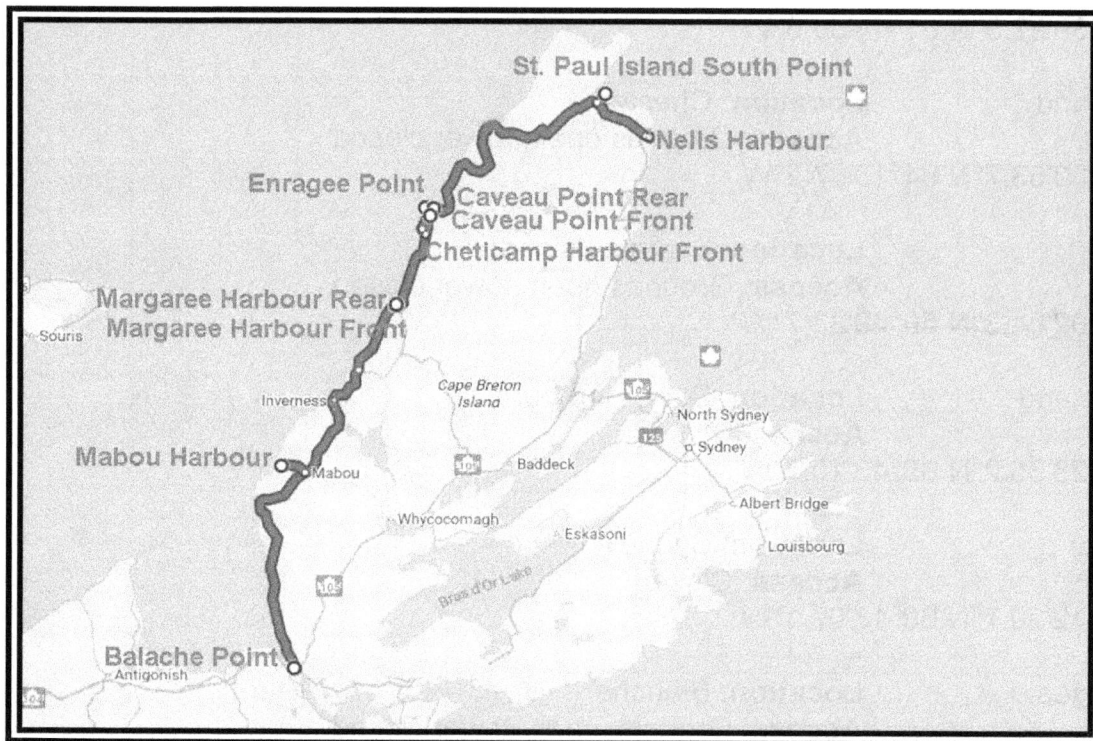

10 lighthouses, 4 hours driving

Balache Point Rear Range	45°38'52.9"N 61°24'51.8"W
Mabou Harbour	46°05'09.2"N 61°27'55.2"W
Margaree Harbour Front Range	46°26'22.6"N 61°06'45.1"W
Margaree Harbour Rear Range	46°26'20.6"N 61°06'44.4"W
Enragee Point	46°38'58.4"N 61°01'35.2"W
Cheticamp Harbour Front Range	46°37'56.8"N 61°00'40.1"W
Caveau Point Front Range	46°38'56.6"N 61°00'6.00"W
Caveau Point Rear Rang	46°38'54.7"N 60°59'51.5"W
St. Paul Island South Point	46°54'02.6"N 60°27'40.0"W
Neils' Harbour	46°48'23.3"N 60°19'11.0"W

Cape Breton Tour2

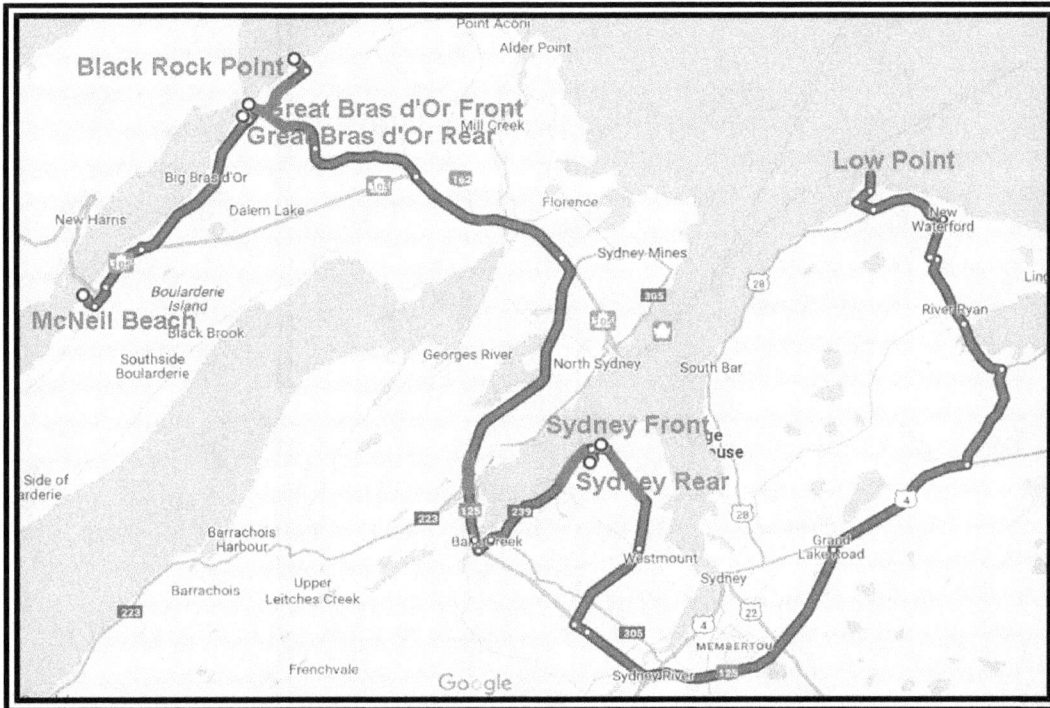

7 lighthouses, 1hour 30 minutes driving

McNeil Beach	46°13'43.2"N 60°29'25.1"W
Great Bras d'Or Rear Range	46°17'12.3"N 60°24'59.1"W
Great Bras d'Or Front Range	46°17'25.5"N 60°24'48.3"W
Black Rock Point	46°18'18.8"N 60°23'31.4"W
Sydney Rear Range	46°10'27.9"N 60°15'20.3"W
Sydney Front Range	46°10'48.2"N 60°15'01.1"W
Low Point	46°16'01.5"N 60°07'32.9"W

Cape Breton Tour3

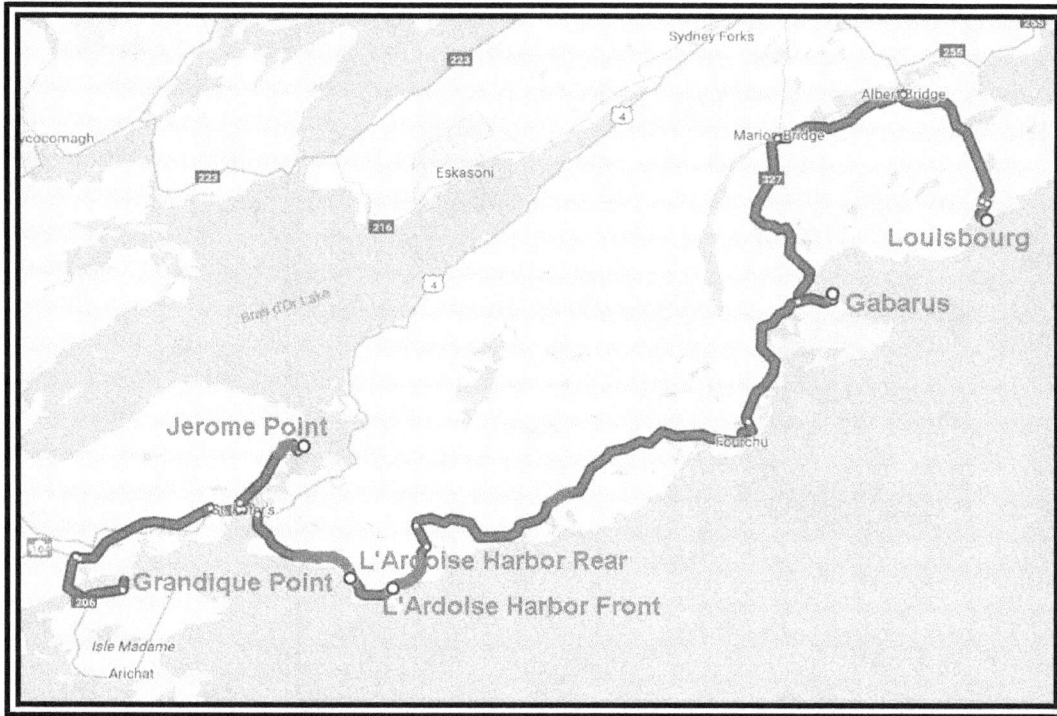

6 lighthouses, 3 hours driving

Louisbourg	45°54'24.0"N 59°57'30.5"W
Gabarus	45°50'36.5"N 60°08'50.5"W
L'Ardoise Harbor Front	45°35'18.1"N 60°41'25.4"W
L'Ardoise Harbor Rear	45°35'48.8"N 60°44'35.0"W
Jerome Point	45°38'53.9"N 60°52'21.8"W
Grandique Point	45°35'38.2"N 61°01'19.8"W

Eastern Shore Tour

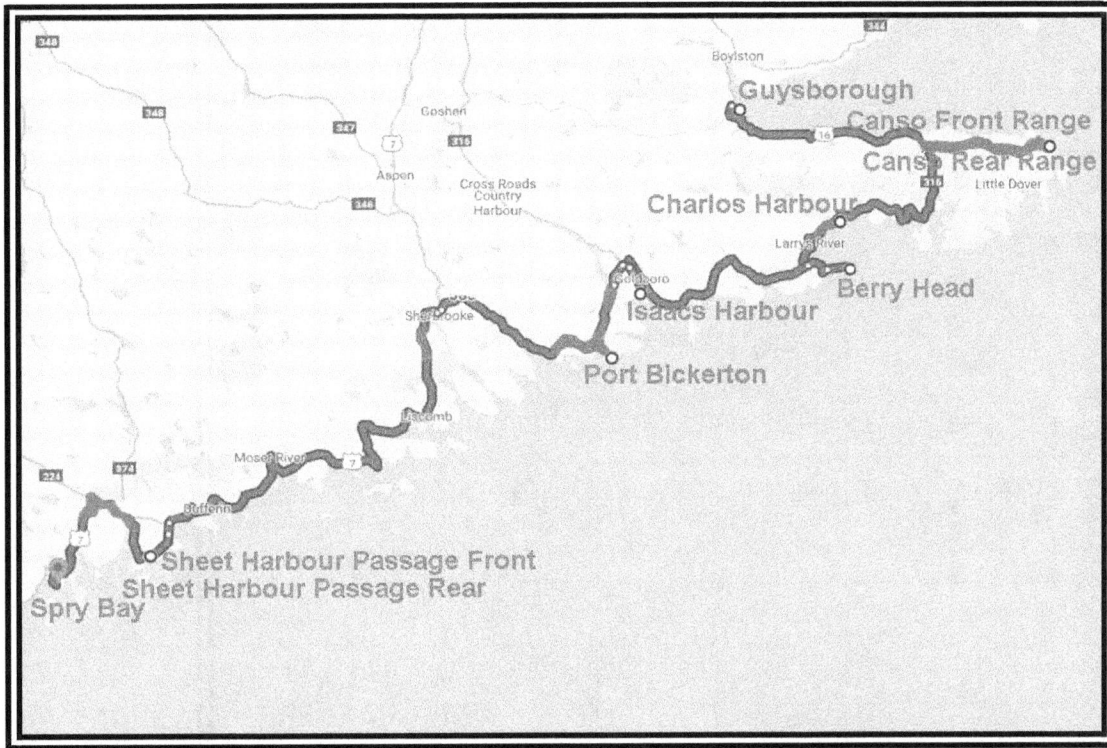

10 lighthouses, 5 hours driving

Guysborough	45°22'39.9"N 61°29'26.7"W
Canso Front Range	45°19'56.2"N 60°58'46.5"W
Canso Rear Range	45°19'55.7"N 60°59'01.4"W
Charlos Harbour Rear Range	45°14'48.3"N 61°19'39.8"W
Berry Head	45°11'28.8"N 61°18'39.9"W
Isaacs Harbour	45°09'52.8"N 61°39'16.5"W
Port Bickerton	45°05'24.0"N 61°42'01.7"W
Sheet Harbour Passage Front Range	44°51'30.0"N 62°26'56.0"W
Sheet Harbour Passage Rear Range	44°51'36.2"N 62°26'58.7"W
Spry Bay	44°49'21.5"N 62°35'54.3"W

Fundy Shore Tour1

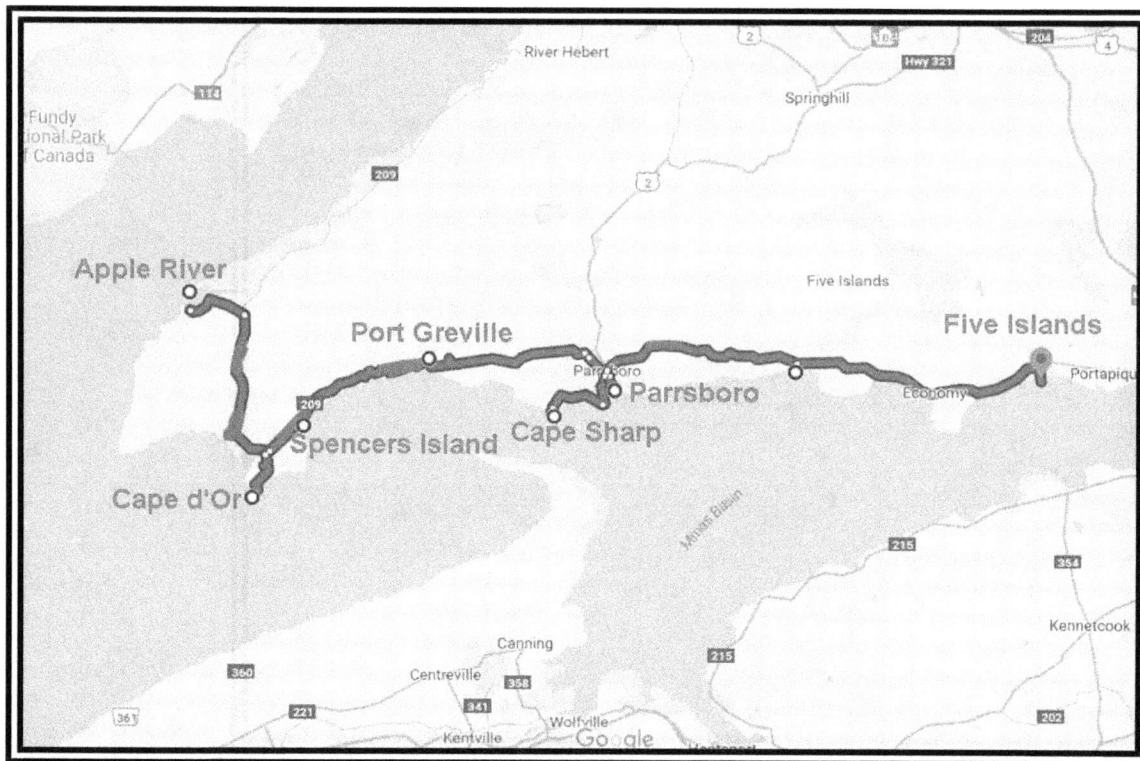

7 Lighthouses, 2 hr 30 minutes driving

Apple River	45°28'25.5"N 64°51'16.9"W
Spencers Island	45°21'17.5"N 64°42'37.3"W
Cape d'Or	45°17'23.7"N 64°46'28.9"W
Port Greville	45°24'54.7"N 64°33'08.5"W
Cape Sharp	45°21'51.9"N 64°23'32.4"W
Parrsboro	45°23'14.6"N 64°18'56.2"W
Five Islands	45°24'15.9"N 64°05'17.3"W

Fundy Shore Tour2

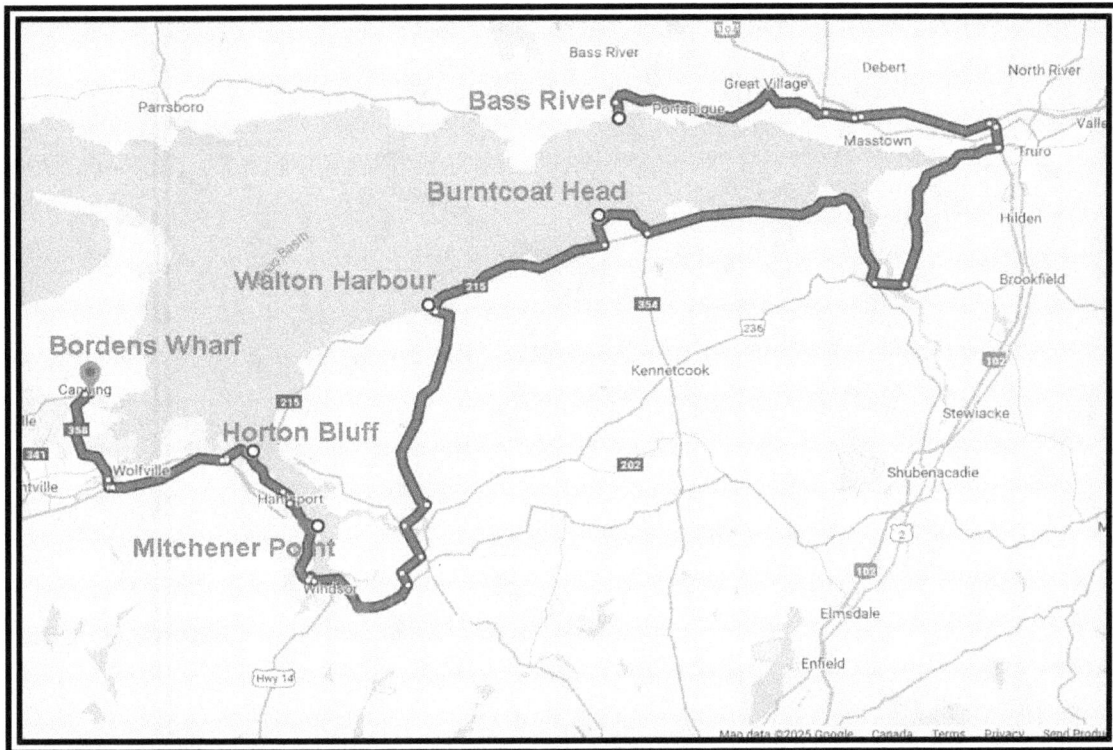

6 Lighthouses, 3 hours driving

Bass River	45°23'42.7"N 63°46'53.2"W
Burntcoat Head	45°18'40.9"N 63°48'21.5"W
Walton Harbour	45°14'03.2"N 64°00'42.9"W
Mitchener Point	45°02'38.0"N 64°08'47.0"W
Horton Bluff	45°06'30.6"N 64°13'31.1"W
Bordens Wharf	45°09'26.5"N 64°25'20.2"W

Fundy Shore Tour3

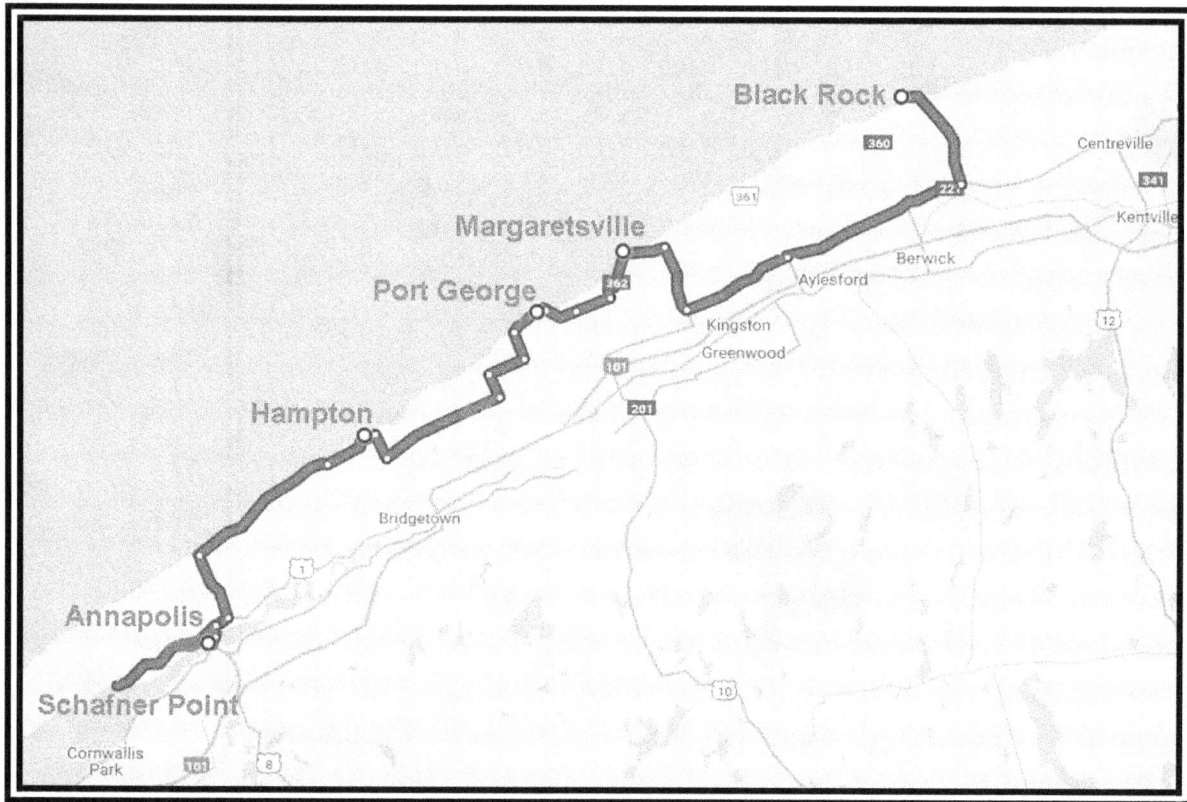

6 Lighthouses, 2 hours driving

Black Rock	45°10'13.2"N 64°45'42.6"W
Margaretsville	45°03'00.3"N 65°03'57.8"W
Port George	45°00'10.8"N 65°09'38.1"W
Hampton	44°54'21.8"N 65°21'00.8"W
Annapolis	44°44'39.6"N 65°31'11.8"W
Schafner Point	44°42'35.5"N 65°37'08.6"W

Halifax Tour

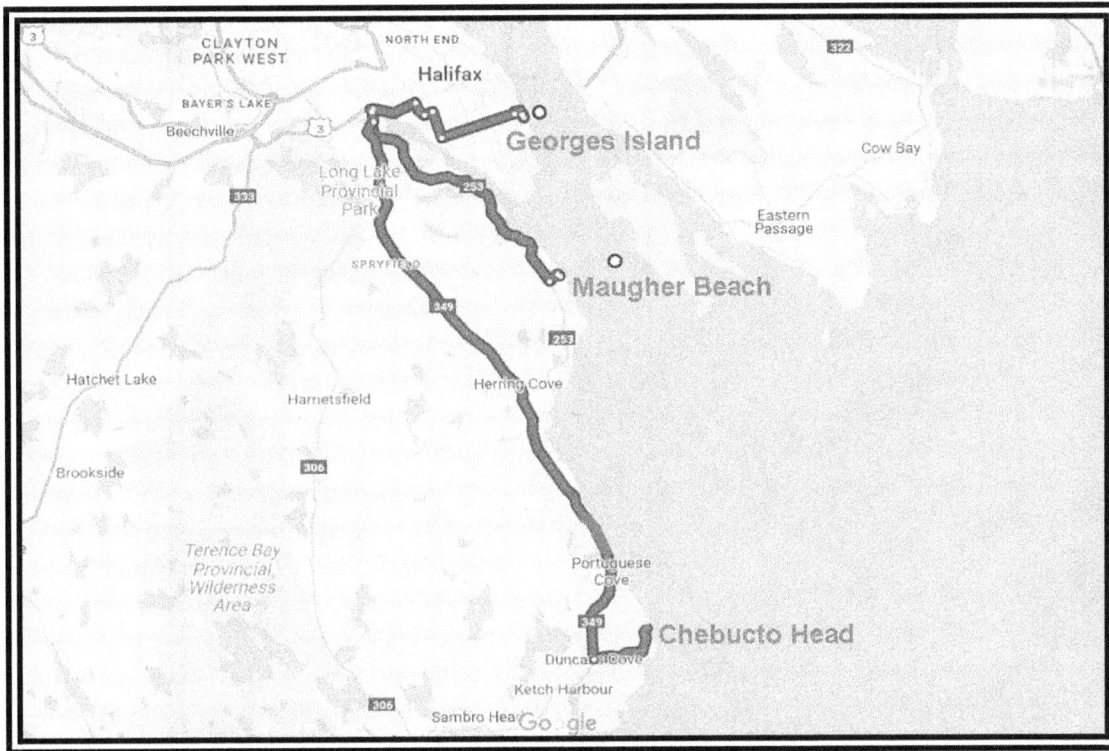

3 Lighthouse, 1 hour driving

Maugher Beach	44°36'07.9"N 63°32'01.0"W
Georges Island	44°38'25.8"N 63°33'37.4"W
Chebucto Head	44°30'26.6"N 63°31'21.4"W

Northumberland Shore Tour1

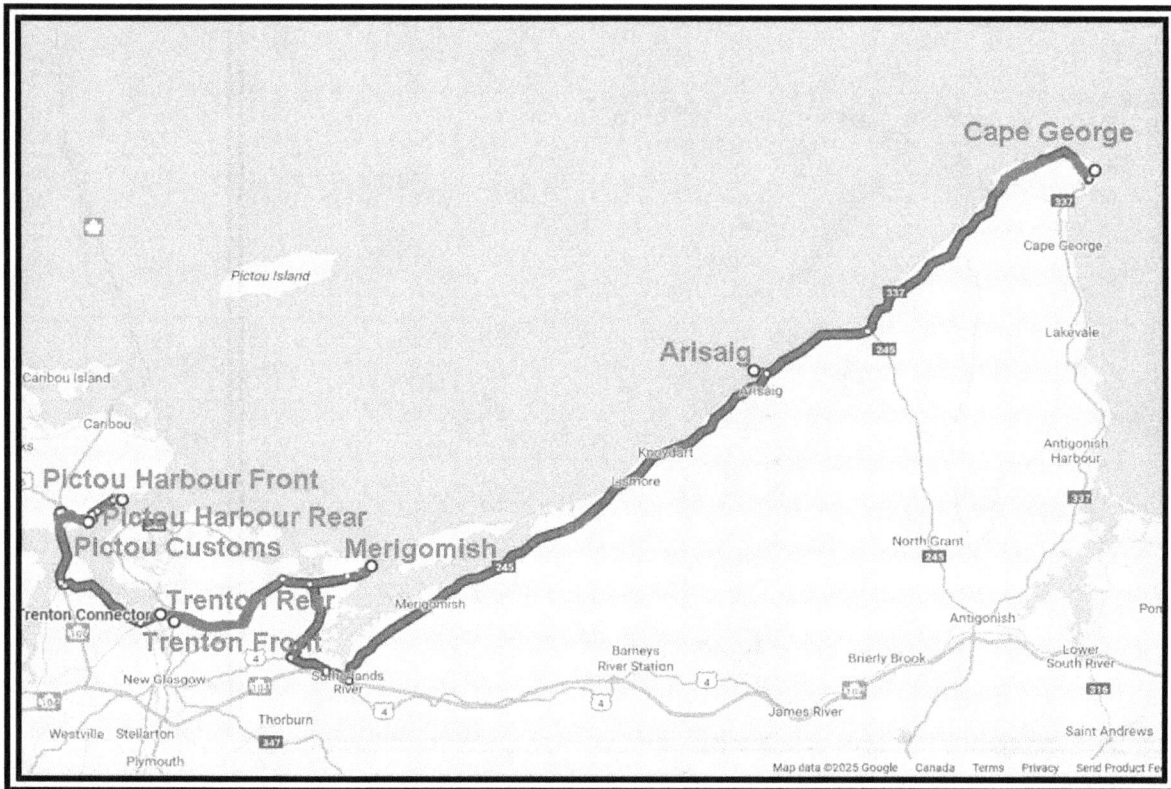

6 Lighthouses, 2 hours 15 minutes driving

Caribou	45°45'53.2"N 62°40'50.3"W
Wallace Harbour Rear Range	45°48'32.0"N 63°17'23.2"W
Wallace Harbour Front Range	45°48'47.2"N 63°27'43.1"W
Mullins Point Rear Range	45°49'27.6"N 63°26'36.3"W
Coldspring Head	45°57'44.7"N 63°51'54.6"W
Woody Point	45°57'51.9"N 63°52'53.2"W

Northumberland Shore Tour2

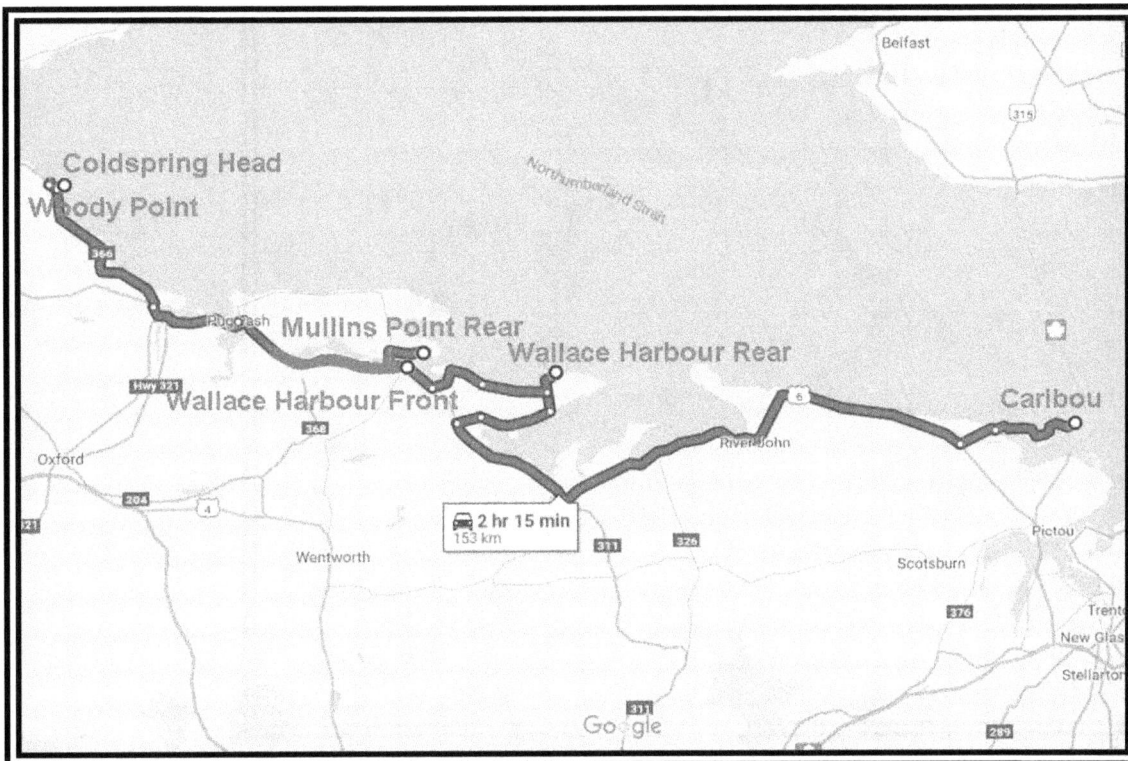

6 Lighthouses, 2 hours 15 minutes driving

Caribou	45°45'53.2"N 62°40'50.3"W
Wallace Harbour Rear Range	45°48'32.0"N 63°17'23.2"W
Wallace Harbour Front Range	45°48'47.2"N 63°27'43.1"W
Mullins Point Rear Range	45°49'27.6"N 63°26'36.3"W
Coldspring Head	45°57'44.7"N 63°51'54.6"W
Woody Point	45°57'51.9"N 63°52'53.2"W

South Shore Tour1

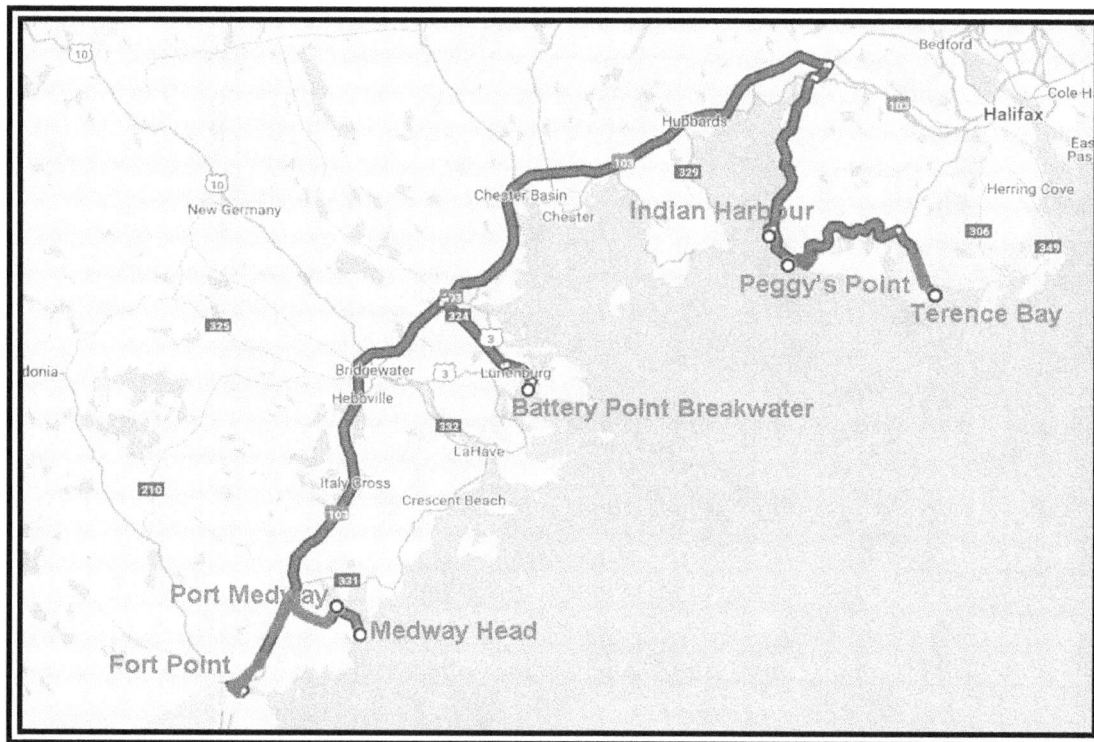

7 Lighthouses, 3 hours 15 minues driving

Terence Bay	44°27'36.6"N 63°42'20.8"W
Peggy's Point	44°29'30.8"N 63°55'08.0"W
Indian Harbour	44°31'19.6"N 63°56'45.3"W
Battery Point Breakwater	44°21'36.8"N 64°17'47.3"W
Port Medway	44°07'55.5"N 64°34'28.4"W
Medway Head	44°06'10.6"N 64°32'23.3"W
Fort Point	44°02'36.6"N 64°42'27.3"W

South Shore Tour2

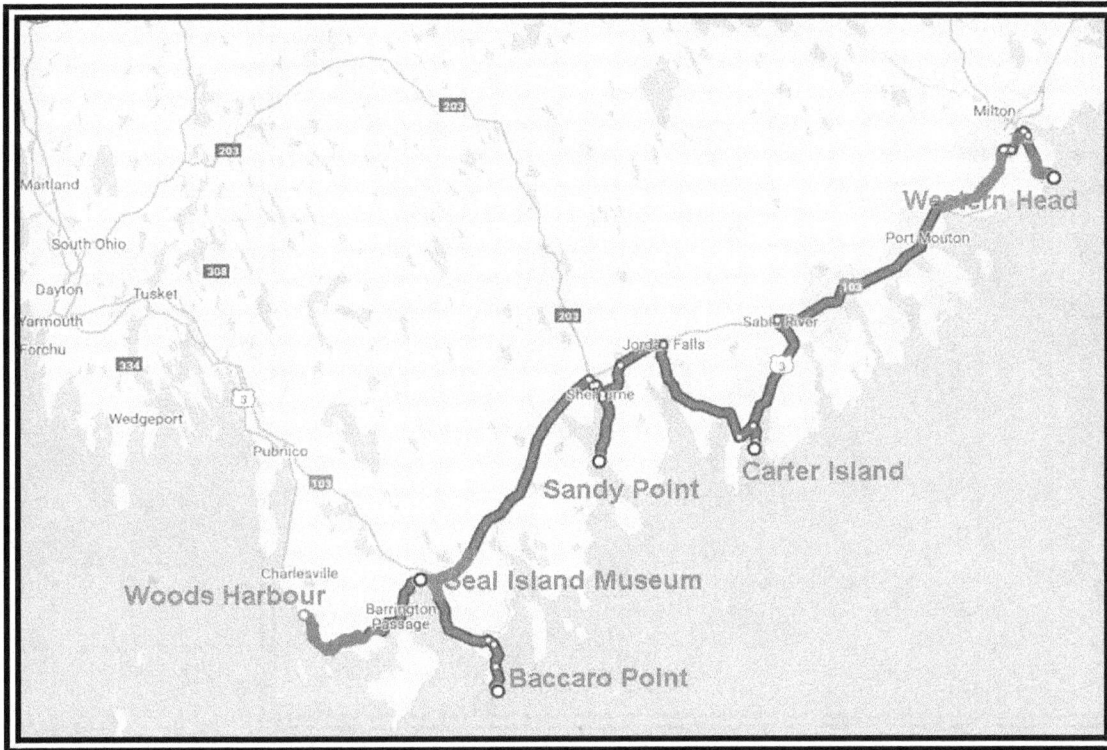

6 Lighthouses, 3 hours driving

Western Head	43°59'20.8"N 64°39'44.5"W
Carter Island	43°42'19.3"N 65°06'04.0"W
Sandy Point	43°41'29.3"N 65°19'31.3"W
Baccaro Point	43°26'59.0"N 65°28'15.0"W
Seal Island Museum	43°34'00.6"N 65°34'50.6"W
Woods Harbour	43°31'10.5"N 65°44'43.1"W

Yarmouth Tour

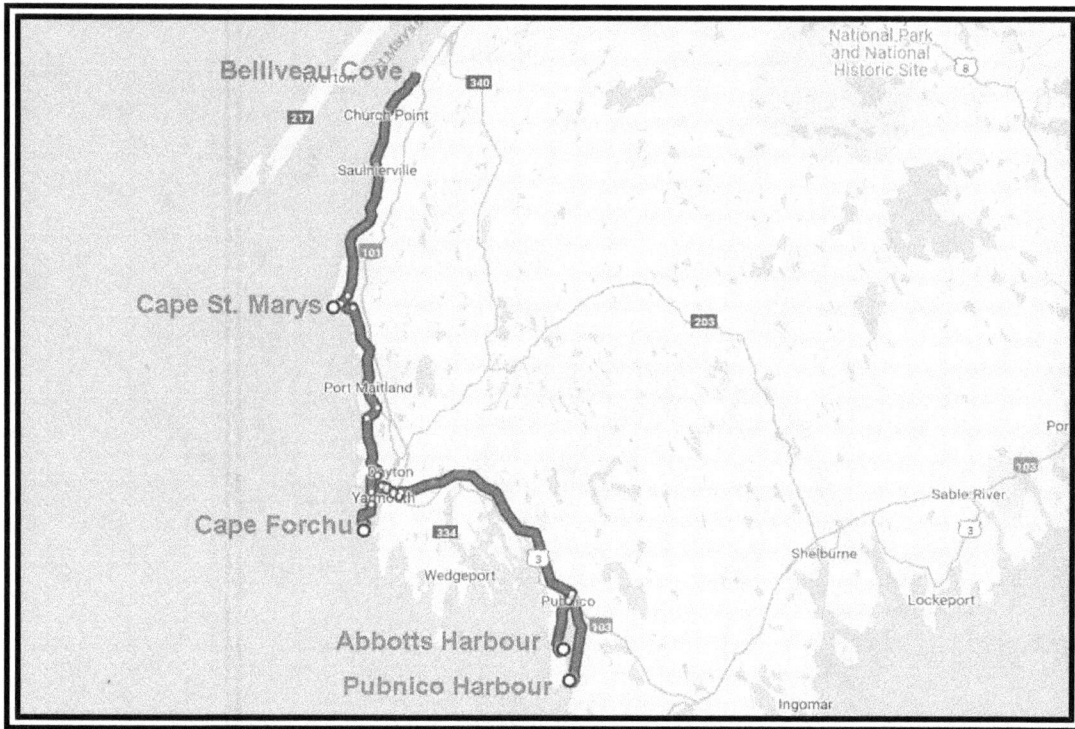

5 Lighthouses, 2 hours 30 minutes driving

Pubnico Harbour	43°35'53.4"N 65°46'55.6"W
Abbotts Harbour	43°38'21.3"N 65°47'34.8"W
Cape Forchu	43°47'38.8"N 66°09'19.3"W
Cape St. Marys	44°05'09.5"N 66°12'39.7"W
Belliveau Cove	44°23'20.4"N 66°03'49.6"W

Glossary of Lighthouse Terms

Aerobeacon: A lighting system which creates a signal over long distances. It consists of a strong light source with a focusing mechanism which is rotated on a vertical axis. It has been used at airports as well as lighthouses.

Acetylene: After 1910, acetylene began to be used to power the lighthouse light source. It has the advantage that it could be stored on site with a sun valve turning it on at dusk and off at daybreak.

Alternating Light: A light source which changes colours in a regular pattern.

Arc of Visibility: The range of the horizon from which the lighthouse is visible from the sea.

Automated: A lighthouse that operates without a keeper. The light functions are controlled by timers, and light and fog detectors.

Beacon: A fixed aid to navigation.

Bell: A sound signal produced by fixed aids and by sea movement on buoys.

Breakwater: A structure that protects a shore area or harbour by blocking waves.

Bull's-eye Lens: A convex lens used to refract light.

Catwalk: An elevated walkway which allows the keeper to move in the lantern room in towers built in the sea.

Characteristic: The distinct pattern of the flashing light or foghorn blast which allows seamen to distinguish which light station it is coming from.

Chariot: A wheeled assembly at the bottom of a Fresnel lens which is rotated around a circular track.

Clockwork Mechanism: Early lighthouses had a series of gears, pulleys and weights, which had to be wound on a recurring basis by the keepers.

Cottage Style Lighthouse: A lighthouse made up of a keeper's residence with a light on top.

Crib: A base structure filled with stone which acted as the foundation for the structure built on top.

Daymark: A unique colour pattern that identifies a specific lighthouse during the day.

Decommissioned: A lighthouse that has discontinued operating as a aid to navigation.

Diaphone: A sound signal produced by a slotted piston moved by compressed air.

Directional Light: A light which marks the direction to be followed.

Eclipse: The interval between light flashed or foghorn blasts.

Fixed Light: A light shining continuously without periods of eclipse or darkness.

Flashing Light: Alight pattern distinguished by periods of eclipse or darkness.

Focal Plane: The path of a beam of light emitted from a lighthouse. The height from the center of the beam to the sea is known as the height of the focal plane.

Fog Detector: A device used to automatically determine conditions which may reduce visibility and the need to start a sound signal.

Fog Signal: An audible device such as a bell or horn that warns seamen during period of fog when the light would be ineffective.

Fresnel Lens: An optic system composed of a convex lens and prisms which concentrate the light beam through a series of prisms. The design was produced by Augustin Fresnel in the 1800s.

Geographic Range: The longest distance the curvature of the earth allows an object of a certain height to be seen.

Isophase Light: A light in which the duration of light and darkness are equal.

Keeper: The person responsible for the maintenance and operation of the lighthouse.

Lamp and Reflector: A lamp and polished mirror used before the invention of more effective optic systems such as the Fresnel lens.

Lantern: A glass covered space at the top of the lighthouse tower, which housed the lighting equipment.

Lens: The glass optical system used to concentrate and direct the light.

Light Sector: The arc over which a light can be seen from the sea.

Lightship: A ship that served as a lighthouse.

Light Station: The lighthouse tower as well as any outbuildings such as the keeper's quarters, fog-signal building, fuel storage building and boathouse.

Nautical Mile: A unit of distance which is the average distance on the Earth's surface represented by one minute of latitude. It is equal to 1.1508 statute miles and mainly used at sea.

Nominal Range: The distance a light can be seen in good weather.

Occulting Light: A light in which the period of light is longer than the period of darkness and in which the intervals of darkness are all equal. Also known as an eclipsing light.

Order: A description of the power of the Fresnel lens ranging from one to seven from stronger to weaker.

Parabolic Reflector: A metal bowl shaped to a parabolic curve which reflects a lamp's light from it's center.

Parapet: A railed walkway which surrounds the lamp room.

Period: The total time for one cycle of the pattern of the light or sound signal.

Pharologist: A person with an interest in lighthouses.

Range Lights: Two lights which form a range provide direction to mariners for safe passage. They are described as the Front and Rear Lighthouses or the Inner and Outer. The front range light is lower than the rear, and when they align,the ship is in the proper position.

Revetment: A bank of stone laid to protect a structure against erosion from waves.

Revolving Light: A flash produced by the rotation of a Fresnel lens.

Riprap: Broken rocks or stone placed to help prevent erosion.

Sector: The portion of the sea lit by a sector light.

Skeleton Tower: Towers consisting of four or more braced feet with a beacon on top. They have little resistance to the wind and waves, and bear up well in a storm.

Solar-powered Optic: Many automated lights are run on solar powered batteries.

Spider Lamp: A brass container holding oil and solid wicks.

Tender: A ship which services lighthouses.

Ventilator: Opening' at the top of a lighthouse tower to provide heat exhaust and air flow within the tower.

Wick Solid: A solid cord which draws fuel to the flame in spider lamps.

Photo Credits

Alessio Damato; A coruna torre de hercules: **Aurora.douthwright**; Burntcoat Head Bardencj; Seal Island: **Burning7Chrome**; Mitchener Point: **Canadian Coast Guard**; Bear River; Coffin Island; Coldspring Head, Green Island, Sable Island: **Dennis Jarvis**; Apple River, Bass River, Berry Head, Bordens Wharf, Cape Sharp; Carter Island, Cranberry Island, Devils Island, East Ironbound Island, Gillis Point, Great Bras D'Or Front, Gull Rock, Jeddore Rock, Jerseyman Island, Marache Point, Margaree Harbour Range, Margaretville, Maugher Beach, McNeril Beach, Merigomish, Monroe Point, Outer Island, Peter Island, Pictou Range, Port Bickerton, Port Moutan, Pubnico Harbour, Queensport, River Bourgeois, Sheet Harbour, Terrence Bay, Victoria Beach, West Head, Westhaver Island, Woody Point: **Gordon Leggett**; Bunker Island: **James Somers**; Cape Forchu: **Jmwharris**; Mabou: **Keith Lehwald**; Georges Island: **Letterofmarque**; Sambro Island: **Magicpiano**; Hampton: **Manfredwinslow**; Cape Sable: **PortGeorgeScribe**; Port George: **Thiersch**; Pharos: **Taxiarchos228;** Battery Point Breakwater

All other images by the author

153

The Photographer's and Explorer's Series

Unless noted, there are Print and eBook editions available for the following.

Birds
Birding Guide to Orkney
Guide to Photographing Birds

Covered Bridges
Alabama Covered Bridges (eBook only)
California Covered Bridges (eBook only)
Canada's Covered Bridges
Connecticut Covered Bridges (eBook only)
Georgia Covered Bridges (eBook only)
Illinois Covered Bridges (eBook only)
Indiana Covered Bridges
Iowa Covered Bridges (eBook only)
Maine Covered Bridges (eBook only)
Massachusetts Covered Bridges (eBook only)
Michigan Covered Bridges (eBook only)
Minnesota Covered Bridge (eBook only)
New Brunswick Covered Bridges
New England Covered Bridges
Covered Bridges of the Mid-Atlantic
Quebec Covered Bridges
Covered Bridges of the South
Missouri Covered Bridges (eBook only)
New Hampshire Covered Bridges
New York Covered Bridges
Ohio's Covered Bridges
Oregon Covered Bridges
The Covered Bridges of Kentucky (eBook only)
The Covered Bridges of Kentucky and Tennessee
The Covered Bridges of Tennessee (eBook only)
Vermont's Covered Bridges
The Covered Bridges of Virginia (eBook only)
The Covered Bridges of Virginia and West Virginia
Washington Covered Bridges (eBook only)
The Covered Bridges of West Virginia (eBook only)
West Coast Covered Bridges
Wisconsin Covered Bridges (eBook only)

Lighthouses
Maine Lighthouses
New Brunswick
Newfoundland Lighthouses
Nova Scotia
Ontario Lighthouses
Orkney and Shetland Lighthouses (eBook only)
Prince Edward Island Lighthouses
Scotland Lighthouses

Old Mills
Ontario's Old Mills

Ontario Waterfalls
Ontario Waterfalls

Index

www.ingramcontent.com/pod-product-compliance
Lightning Source LLC
Chambersburg PA
CBHW080517090426
42734CB00015B/3084